# Top 20 Teachers

## The Revolution in American Education

Paul Bernabei  Tom Cody    Willow Sweeney
Mary Cole   Michael Cole

Designed and Illustrated by Tim Parlin

Top 20 Press
An Imprint of Morgan James Publishing
St. Paul, MN • New York, NY

# TOP 20 TEACHERS

## The Revolution in American Education

by Paul Bernabei, Tom Cody, Willow Sweeney
© 2010 Paul Bernabei, Tom Cody, Willow Sweeney. All rights reserved.

ISBN 978-0-97428-432-3 (paperback)

**Published by:**

## TOP 20 PRESS

*an imprint of*
Morgan James Publishing, LLC
1225 Franklin Ave. Ste 325
Garden City, NY 11530-1693
Toll Free 800-485-4943
www.MorganJamesPublishing.com

In an effort to support local communities, raise awareness and funds, Morgan James Publishing donates one percent of all book sales for the life of each book to Habitat for Humanity.
Get involved today, visit **www.HelpHabitatForHumanity.org.**

# ABOUT THE AUTHORS

The authors of this book have been on a wonderful journey. Paul Bernabei, Tom Cody, Willow Sweeney, Mary Cole and Michael Cole have enjoyed a decade of working together and growing professionally and personally.

They formed Top 20 Training in 2002 to provide training and materials to help youth and adults develop their potential. Over the last five years, they have trained over 25,000 teachers throughout the United States. They have co-authored *Top 20 Teens: Discovering the Best-kept Thinking, Learning and Communicating Secrets of Successful Teenagers* (now in its third printing) and *Top 20 Parents: Raising Happy, Responsible and Emotionally Healthy Children* (2009). The Top 20 curriculum they have created is now implemented in hundreds of grade schools, middle schools, high schools and alternative learning programs. The authors have presented at numerous state and national educational and leadership conferences.

Paul Bernabei directs Top 20 Training. He has been a teacher, counselor, administrator and coach in Twin Cities grade schools and high schools for 32 years. Paul also directs Share-A-Life, a program that provides housing and support for pregnant women in crisis. A graduate of St. John's University and the University of St. Thomas, Paul and his wife, Paula, a kindergarten teacher, reside in St. Paul, Minnesota. They have four daughters and eight grandchildren.

Tom Cody has been a grade school and high school math teacher since 1974. He has been instrumental in developing innovative curriculum programs at Cretin-Derham Hall High School where he has also coached several athletic teams and taught TLC: Thinking Learning and Communicating since 2000. A graduate of Colorado State University, Tom and his wife, Judy, a fifth grade teacher, reside in St. Paul, Minnesota. They have three sons.

Willow Sweeney has been a high school social studies teacher and coach. She has taught TLC: Thinking Learning and Communicating classes as well as world cultures and social justice. Her work with Top 20 Training focuses on communication and relationship topics. Her exceptional ability to build rapport with students helps make Top 20 concepts immediately relevant to their lives. Willow and her husband, Brian, live in St. Cloud, Minnesota. They have two children.

Mary Cole is the co-founder and vice-president of Salon Development Corporation. For the last 24 years, she has developed materials, programs and products provided by her company. She facilitates training sessions with Michael, her husband and business partner. Mary helped create the original Top 20 curriculum for students and has taught for three years.

Michael Cole has been a seminar educator for 34 years. He is founder and president of Salon Development Corporation, an international company specializing in business training. He is a world-renowned recipient of numerous awards for helping thousands of professionals transform their lives. The Coles live in St. Paul, Minnesota. They have two children and two grandchildren.

# ACKNOWLEDGMENTS

We have been blessed by people who care. Throughout our lives, family members, friends and colleagues have supported us with encouragement and patience. We are grateful for their love.

We have been blessed by teachers. Throughout our schooling, mentors and coaches have believed in our potential, helped us develop our skills and talent, and taught us important life lessons. We are grateful for their dedication and wisdom.

We have been blessed by students. Throughout our careers, young people have come desiring to learn, to grow and to be valued. We are grateful for their curiosity and their needs.

We have been blessed by people who have shared their stories in this book. Some of them are named but many are not. We are grateful for their willingness to make this book real and better.

All of these people have been role models for us. They have awakened in us compassion and a desire to make a positive difference in the lives of others. We are grateful for the spirit to serve.

Finally, we have been blessed by the next generation. They are waiting and longing for something more. They remind us of the future that is still to be created. We are grateful for the inspiration they have given us to write this book.

*Top 20 Teachers* is filled with stories, some from our imagination and some from our own lives. Throughout the book, we will use our first names whenever referring to our own stories or personal experiences. All factual stories are designated by a True Tales icon.

In order to avoid the use of he/she, we have chosen to alternate gender pronouns.

Dear Reader,

It is the beginning of a new day in Minnesota...a cold day but the sun is shining. It is a day of promise and hope.

Within a few miles of our homes are more than 30 schools: colleges, high schools, alternative schools, middle schools, trade schools and elementary schools. Driving through our neighborhood to begin work on this book, we pass thousands of students...many in buses, some being driven by their parents, others walking with friends...on their way to school. What will happen in the lives of these young people?

The answer to that question comes in the form of four other questions:

1. What will be given to them today?
2. What will be taken from them today?
3. What will be discovered in them today?
4. What will be developed in them today?

The answers to these questions will affect the lives of young people and our nation for decades to come. In other words, **whatever is taking place in the schools in our neighborhoods and throughout our country is important.**

These four questions can be answered in many ways. This book looks at one way of answering these tremendously important questions: **it depends on the teachers the students encounter in schools today.**

What will teachers give students today?

Some will give their students information and assignments.
Others will give their students hope and encouragement.

What will teachers take from students today?

Some will take their students' curiosity and spirit.
Others will take their false beliefs and roadblocks to success.

What will teachers discover in students today?

Some will discover in their students boredom and apathy.
Others will discover a desire to make a positive difference in their lives.

What will teachers develop in students today?

Some will develop negativity in their students.
Others will develop Star Qualities in their students that will enrich their lives.

What is being given, taken, discovered or developed in a school matters. The development or diminishment of human life is what is going on in school today.

We have written this book because we want people to know that what goes on in schools is terribly important. We want people who have influence in schools—students, teachers, parents, administrators, counselors, coaches, support staff, school board members, policy makers, tax payers and grandparents—to take seriously and be concerned about the terribly important things that are going on in schools today.

Therefore, this book is dangerous.

A revolution is needed in our schools today. Only the Rip Van Winkles who have been asleep for the last 20 years would be unaware of that. This book attempts to fuel that revolution…but to fuel it in a manner that directs the energy of this revolution to empower youth and teachers to make a positive difference in their lives.

## THE BELIEF IN POSSIBILITIES

The fundamental power behind this revolution is the belief in possibilities. As such it is a revolution rooted deeply in the American spirit, a spirit that is wise in taking what needs to be preserved, courageous to adventure across a challenging frontier, dependent on the companionship and hospitality of fellow travelers and drawn forward by the dream of a prosperous new land.

Americans have always believed in possibilities. That belief fueled the creative spirit of inventors and the adventuresome spirit of pioneers who journeyed across the Continental Divide in covered wagons and the galaxies in space ships. It fueled the spirit of sacrifice by men and women in our armed forces and countless people of all colors who tirelessly worked and died for civil rights. This belief in possibilities is at the core of who we are as a people. It is our passion. It is what we live for. It is our legacy to our own children and to our world.

Today in our neighborhood and in your neighborhood children are on their way to school. They are sent there because parents believe in possibilities. They hope for what is best for their children. This book seeks to partner our sacred vocation as teachers with the deep desire of parents and the needs of children to create new possibilities. **It seeks to provide each student with a Top 20 Teacher.**

## THE ROLE OF A TEACHER

Years ago the role of the teacher was to put content into the heads of students what was either in the teacher's head or in a book. Clearly, a teacher was a transmitter of information.

The night before Paul taught his first class of American literature to high school juniors in 1970, his sole concern was to prepare himself by getting enough in his head so he could spill it into theirs. Within seconds of the bell ringing to begin class the next morning, his students sat quietly knowing what to expect. Being faithful to the task, he unscrewed their heads and poured in the information that had been poured into his own head.

His students sat quietly and wrote in their notebooks what he was saying. He had good students and he was a good teacher. He continued this practice of passing on knowledge to his students for many years.

One day he noticed that a student didn't have his notebook. After a few weeks that number grew. Some students even forgot to bring their books to class. Their test scores declined. They became more and more resistant to Paul's unscrewing their heads. They actually began talking to each other rather than listening to him. Grades got worse and a few students even failed his class. He no longer had good students.

Unbeknownst to him, thus began the revolution in American education. His students had begun to pour tea into Boston harbor: **No education without participation.** His students had a good teacher. What they needed was a Top 20 teacher.

The purpose of this book is to support the revolution initiated by students in American schools. In various ways, students are telling us that they need something different if the potential waiting in them is going to come forth and make a positive difference in their lives and in their world. In an effort to give them hope that something wonderful is possible, we acknowledge having heard their cry for revolution and commit to helping our teaching profession guide and direct the revolution to a successful outcome.

## SCHOOL: A TERRIBLY IMPORTANT PLACE

School is a place of wonder and fear, discovery and disappointment, belonging and estrangement, hope and despair. It is a peaceful place where friendships are founded and a war zone where lives are lost. It is a place youngsters enjoy…where they play and learn and develop and contribute. It is a place youngsters hate…where they ache and get stuck and quit and lash out.

School is terribly important because it is a place to which all kids come and spend a great deal of time. It is a terribly important place whether children experience wonder, discovery, belonging and hope or fear, disappointment, estrangement and despair. It is terribly important to each of them individually and it is terribly important to us as a people now and for generations to come.

Each day in this place called school, children meet some terribly important people called teachers. Whether they meet this teacher in a classroom or a lunchroom, an office or a playground, a bus or a gymnasium, every meeting is terribly important. Every encounter between a student and a teacher creates a possibility for learning. What the child learns in that encounter is important for that child's life now and well into his or her future.

Teaching is a serious profession. Who we are and what we do make a difference, a terribly important difference, in the lives of children and in the life of our nation. Consequently, we need to be aware of what is going on in our students and in ourselves. **Awareness is the fuel of this revolution.**

As crucial as awareness is for this revolution, it is not sufficient. Paul Revere was not only aware that the British were coming, he communicated it. He rode throughout the countryside to let others know.

*Top 20 Teachers* supports this revolution for what is in the best interest of children by inviting our teaching profession to become more aware of what's really going on in students and in ourselves and communicating that to each other. By this awareness and discussion new possibilities will emerge.

Thank you for choosing to teach America's youth and for wanting to make a positive difference in their lives. Thank you for wanting to be a Top 20 teacher.

Sincerely,

Paul Bernabei, Tom Cody, Willow Sweeney, Mary Cole and Michael Cole

# Table of Contents

# Part 1:
# Teaching America's Youth

# CHAPTER 1

## TOP 20 TEACHERS

# Have Power to Make a Positive Difference

As a youngster, Paul would often travel with his grandfather across a bridge that spanned the Illinois River. Whenever they came to this place, Paul noticed a quiet smile on his grandfather's face. One day Paul asked, "Grampa, why do you smile whenever we come to this bridge?"

"My boy," the old man responded, "grampa built this bridge. Whenever we pass by, I think of the many people this bridge has helped. I also remember the men who worked with me and the enjoyable time we had together."

Like Paul's grandfather, teachers are builders. They build relationships that enable students to reach new places, places where they experience their own discoveries and opportunities to grow and create.

This book is about power. More specifically, it is about the power a teacher has to make a difference in students' lives.

## SUCCESS = GR + GR

Unbeknownst to Paul at the time, his grandfather was explaining to him the definition of success in the workplace:

### Success = Great Results + Great Ride

Great Results are those outcomes we desire when we go to work each day. For Paul's grandfather, the Great Result was the bridge itself. For teachers, those results include our students learning the lessons we have prepared and becoming life-long learners as well as our getting a paycheck and health benefits every two weeks. We work because we desire good things for others and good things for ourselves.

Great Ride means we want to enjoy the experience. We want to enjoy what we do and have meaningful relationships with our colleagues. We wouldn't consider it a great success if we attained great results in our work but hated going to school every day. Nor would it be a great success if we enjoyed hanging out at school every day but never accomplished anything worthwhile. Years after retirement, as we drive by the schools where we worked, we would like smiles to emanate from our faces as we recall the results and ride we experienced during our years of teaching.

Teachers have the power to make this happen for themselves. They also have the power to make this happen in their students' lives. In essence, **teachers have power to activate the potential in their students to make a positive difference in their lives.**

## STAGES OF POTENTIAL

Teachers need to carry a deep belief in the potential of their students. This belief is the basis of our desire to teach. We teach because we believe in the potential of each student and want to help her develop that potential.

What is potential? Think of a young child. Within this child lies potential…a power inside that waits and waits and waits to get activated so it can make a positive difference in the life, relationships and experiences of the child and, in doing so, make a positive difference in the lives of others as well.

> **Potential is a power in each person**
> **that wants to make a positive difference.**

What happens to that potential over time? For many people nothing happens to it. They have undeveloped potential that remains dormant year after year. These people are represented on the graph by the dotted line.

For many people their potential develops at a rate that would be commonly expected. They are achieving reasonable goals and getting along fine with others. They are represented by the broken line.

But for some people, their potential explodes. They experience Great Results and a Great Ride. They are represented by the solid line.

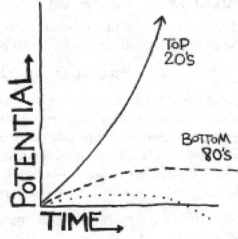

# TOP 20s/BOTTOM 80s AND TLC

We will call the people on the solid line the Top 20 and those on the bottom two lines the Bottom 80. What makes the difference? When we are operating as a Top 20, we Think, Learn and Communicate (TLC) differently than when we are operating as a Bottom 80. When we are Thinking, Learning and Communicating as a Top 20, we are more effective than when we are Thinking, Learning and Communicating as a Bottom 80.

Let's consider an example. Imagine checking your voice mail at the busiest and most hectic time of the day. The first message is from an angry parent and sounds something like this:

> "This is Marge…Billy's mother…Billy told me what happened in class yesterday…I am so mad that you said what you did…he now says he hates history and that used to be his favorite class…he had the best social studies teacher last year and now he hates it…I'm just furious and need to come up there immediately and talk to you about this."

Most of us would immediately feel angry and defensive. However, we have a choice about how we might handle this. We could respond by calling back and leaving this message:

> "Marge, I received your message and would like to listen to your concern. Like you, I want Billy to have the best experience possible in my class. Please come to my classroom after school when I will have some time to discuss how we can best make this happen."

Although we may have been angry when leaving this message, our Top 20 thinking and communicating were highly effective.

A Bottom 80 response might sound more like this:

> "Marge, got your message but I don't think you have a clue about what happened in class yesterday. In fact, I don't know if Billy had a clue about what happened yesterday since he spent the whole class goofing off in the back of the room. Every kid you send here is a pain in the neck. Guess the apple doesn't fall far from the tree, huh, Marge?"

Responding to Marge in this way would result in her next phone call being made to the principal. Bottom 80 thinking and communicating not only fails to solve problems but also serves to make them worse.

**The Top 20 and Bottom 80 labels in this book are not intended to be a comparison between people. Rather, they are simply a way of understanding two dimensions of our own selves.** Sometimes we Think, Learn and Communicate in highly effective Top 20 ways and sometimes in highly ineffective Bottom 80 ways.

**We are all Top 20s.**

**We are all Bottom 80s.**

## IQ or EQ

For years as teachers we tried to raise our students' IQs. The belief that we can do that may be a myth. Regardless of our efforts, whatever our students' true IQs may have been when they started our class is probably what it was when they finished our class.

However, we can help our students improve their EQs. We are able to increase their Emotional Quotient, their awareness of self and others, by helping them discover their internal power to think, learn and communicate in more effective ways.

Many students appear to have a low IQ. Often what presents itself as a low IQ is really a higher IQ that is smothered by negative EQ. By helping our students transform their negative EQs to more positive EQs, their truer higher IQs begin to emerge.

## BEWARE OF THE LIE

Within our educational system, countless students have come to believe that success in life is determined by IQ. If they have high IQs and do well in school, they are guaranteed a successful future.

**Success = High IQ**

This belief is challenged by what really happens in life.

Lets use a bicycle metaphor. The back tire represents a person's IQ. We might think of this as *book smarts* or *school smarts*. The front tire represents EQ, *self smarts* and *people smarts*. Although it's great to have an abundance of book or school smarts, where the bicycle ends up has more to do with the

front tire than the back tire. **Success in life has more to do with a person's awareness of self and other people than it has to do with knowledge of academic subjects.**

This suggests a new formula for success:

**Success = IQ x EQ**

Let's consider some hypothetical examples of this:

**Example 1:** Sally is bright (IQ = 8) and has her hand up all the time. She is arrogant, boastful and irritates people. Sally lacks self-awareness and people skills (EQ = 2). Her success total is only 16.

$$8 \times 2 = 16$$

**Example 2:** Meanwhile, behind Sally sits Andy who has average brainpower (IQ = 5). Andy never gets A's and struggles to get B's and C's. He is dependable, trustworthy and brings out the best in others (EQ = 8). His success total is 40, more than double Sally's.

$$5 \times 8 = 40$$

This is a source of hope for many students: "You mean I can be successful in life even if I don't have the top grades in my class?" Yes, and many students with top grades, unless they have also developed their EQs, will not be successful in life.

Bottom 80 teachers are concerned solely with their students' back tires. They help to perpetuate the lie that success results from only high IQ. Some high achieving Bottom 80 students will be the first hired by businesses and organizations. However, their supervisors will soon discover that they can't work effectively with other people and their negativity drains creative energy from the group. They need to be placed in a room where they work by themselves or be the first fired.

Conversely, people who try their hardest in school, but only achieve average grades, may succeed in business, community and interpersonal relationships if they have a good sense of self and know how to communicate well with others.

Sometimes we encounter students who appear unwilling to participate in the educational process. Their EQs are so negative that teachers become frustrated and often give up on them. In these extreme cases, it is helpful to remember the story of Michelangelo. Before this famous artist began work on his statue of David, he wanted the finest marble possible. However, all that was available was discarded slabs of marble that had been rejected from a construction project. From this inferior marble Michelangelo produced one of the finest pieces of art in history. When asked how he did it, Michelangelo explained that David was in the marble, and he carved away everything that wasn't David.

We can do the same thing with many of the difficult, disengaged young learners we face each day. Sometimes our job is to remove the negative parts life has attached to them that have covered up the radiant reality of who they are.

Top 20 teachers are concerned about their students' back tire but equally focus on pumping up their front tire. They realize that where their students finally end up in life will have more to do with their EQs than IQs.

**Top 20 teachers have power. They have power to activate the potential in their students.** They have power to awaken in their students more effective ways of Thinking, Learning and Communicating. They have power to enrich their students' EQ and, in doing so, help to bring out their true IQ.

The following chapters show how Top 20 teachers use that power to make a positive difference in their own lives, in their students and in their schools.

# TIME FOR REFLECTION & ACTION

1. How would you describe the Great Results you desire as a teacher? How would you describe the Great Ride you desire?

2. What are examples of your Thinking, Learning or Communicating in highly effective Top 20 ways? Of your highly ineffective Bottom 80 ways?

3. What message are you sending to students about what it takes to be successful?

4. What did you become aware of while reading this chapter regarding an action you would like to take? What action would you like to take?

# CHAPTER 2

# TOP 20 TEACHERS
# Know How to
# See Things Differently

While Mr. Lee was giving a spelling test to his third grade class, he noticed Chad sitting in the back row with an open dictionary. After announcing "rainbow," the next word to be spelled, Mr. Lee quietly walked to the back of the room. Standing behind Chad, he saw the dictionary opened to the 'F' section and said, "Chad, can you help me understand why you have an open dictionary during a spelling test?"

"Mr. Lee," said Chad, looking up from the book, "you always ask us to put the date on our papers. I'm not sure how to spell February so I was looking it up."

Seeing a student with an open dictionary, a teacher is likely to believe that the student is cheating. That thought certainly crossed Mr. Lee's mind and was the reason he quietly walked to the back of the room. However, before making a final judgment, he asked Chad a question. The student's answer resulted in the teacher seeing the situation differently.

Teachers make hundreds of judgments each day. Although normally unknown to teachers, the beliefs that form from these judgments have a powerful impact on the teachers' and their students' learning experiences. Being aware of this, Top 20 teachers understand the Frame and how to use it to get better results for themselves and their students.

## THE FRAME

The Frame is a simple but powerful concept. It suggests that how we SEE something (how we think about it; our beliefs, perceptions or opinions) influences how we feel; how we FEEL influences what we do (our behavior or actions); what we DO influences what we get (the results); and typically what we GET reinforces how we see it.

Let's consider a hypothetical example. Imagine that it's a beautiful day and we are walking in the woods. All of a sudden we see a hungry tiger. Seeing the tiger would result in our feeling fear, a feeling that is quite real. That feeling would probably motivate us to run and seek safety.

But what if that particular tiger is a pet of the people in a nearby village. The children play with it and ride on its back. However, we don't know that it is a pet. Still feeling real fear, we would run to get away from the tiger.

Now let's imagine this tiger is really a cardboard cutout of a life-like tiger. This cutout is in the shadows of the trees. Unaware that it is a cardboard cutout, we, believing it is a real tiger, would again feel real fear and try to escape the tiger.

Here are three different situations (a hungry tiger, a pet tiger and a cardboard tiger) that all result in the same *feeling* (fear) and the same *doing* (running to get away). The lesson in this is that it doesn't matter what *it* is. **What matters is how we *see* it.** In all three cases of this example, we saw the object as a threat. Seeing it as a threat, even when it's not, results in our feeling fear.

Top 20s understand that. They realize that what they are getting out of life or a certain experience has to do with how they are seeing it. Bottom 80s would claim that what they are getting out of life has to do with something external: their spouse, their boss, their students or their environment.

In all three parts of this example, the feeling of fear is real. As human beings, we are sometimes fooled into thinking that if what we are feeling is real then what we are seeing must be real. Sometimes it is, but sometimes it's not. If we trust our feelings exclusively, we will sometimes be led to results that are far less than what we are capable of attaining.

Let's consider a more realistic example that we might hear from a student: "My teacher hates me."

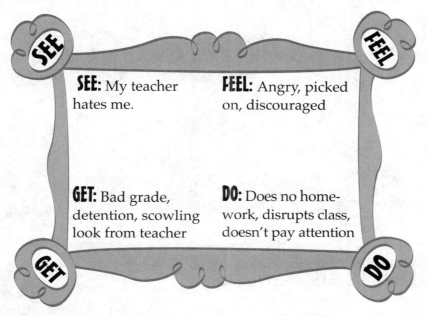

**SEE:** My teacher hates me.

**FEEL:** Angry, picked on, discouraged

**GET:** Bad grade, detention, scowling look from teacher

**DO:** Does no home-work, disrupts class, doesn't pay attention

The results, of course, would reinforce what the student is seeing: "See, I told you my teacher hates me!"

# BASIC CHANGE MODEL

Consider the story of a husband being invited by his wife to her family reunion. He dreads the thought of spending three days with the in-laws and voices his feelings to his wife, "Do I *have* to go to this thing with you?"

"No," says his wife, "you don't *have* to go if you don't want to go. You should only go if you *want* to support me and my family."

Begrudgingly, the husband loads up the car, goes to the reunion and pouts the entire weekend. Although invited by the family to join in games and activities, he sits alone under a shade tree, reads books and ignores the in-laws. His Frame gets him a miserable time. All the way home, he reminds his wife that he was right about having a terrible time. It's as if he rubs the magic lamp, brings out the genie and makes his wish for a terrible time at the reunion. The genie readily complies and the man gets his wish granted.

Five years later he receives a second invitation to attend the next reunion with his wife's in-laws. This time, however, he makes the conscious decision to see the trip differently. "I will be the purveyor of all things fun at this get-together," he announces to himself. At the reunion, he prepares two of the dinners, orders a sight-seeing bus and provides awards for all the games he organizes. On the way home, he tells his wife what a great time he had. The genie is back but this time with different results.

## RESPONSES TO NOT GETTING DESIRED RESULTS

If we are getting the results we want to be *getting*, we should keep *doing* what we are doing, *feeling* how we are feeling, and *seeing* it how we have been seeing it. But what do we do if we are not getting the results we would like to be getting? Like the husband, we can use the Frame as a basic change model.

Top 20s and Bottom 80s respond quite differently when they are not getting the results they want to be getting. The following are three common Bottom 80 responses.

1. **Change nothing.** Bottom 80s change nothing but expect things to get better.

    > Willow enjoyed teaching her third hour class. The only student that challenged her was Maggie, who sat in the back row and sneered at everything Willow did. Willow decided not to do anything about this situation but hoped things would get better in a few days. Maggie's scowling continued and made Willow even more annoyed.

2. **Change what we 'Do'.** Bottom 80s believe that if they change what they do they will change what they get. This is logical and sometimes works. However, if we only change what we do, the change will be small and short-lived.

    > Willow decided to be especially kind to Maggie. Every day for a week, she gave a friendly greeting to Maggie as she entered the classroom. Maggie would return a warm greeting and smile. She would even say, "Hi, Miss Sweeney," whenever she saw Willow in the hall or lunchroom. But the scowling in class continued.

3. **Blame.** The clearest indication that we are operating as a Bottom 80, however, is revealed when we blame someone or something when we are not getting the results we desire. As common as blame is, it is totally dysfunctional. Whether we are aware of it or not, **whenever we blame, we give up power to make a positive difference in our life.** Because we don't take any responsibility, we pass power to someone else and can stay *stuck in yuck* for a long time.

    > Willow decided she had done everything she could to create a positive experience for Maggie. If Maggie wasn't going to change her behavior, it was her fault. She could sit there and pout during third period for the rest of the year. Willow frequently complained to colleagues about this situation but she was done making any effort to make things better.

We always ask teachers during our training if they have ever blamed. They all raise their hands. When we then ask if anyone has ever gotten anything wonderful as a result of blaming, no one raises his hand. Why do we blame so readily when we don't get anything of value in return? That's an interesting question. We believe the answer is that **we blame because we have a need to be right.** When we are not getting the results we want to be getting, our need to be right gets activated and comes out in the form of blame.

If we dig deeper into our need to be right, we might discover a fear of being wrong or not good enough. We will deal with this in Chapter 5.

Bottom 80s are frequently unaware of their need to be right and their tendency to blame. Because they can blame in very subtle and quiet ways, they are often totally unaware of when they are doing it. Nonetheless, whether aware of it or not, they will give up power, feel like a victim and stay *stuck in yuck*.

Let's continue with this example of Willow and Maggie to see how a Top 20 might respond when not getting the results she desires. Top 20s understand that *See* is the most powerful corner of the Frame. They know that what they are *getting* is the result of how they are *seeing*. Consequently, when they are not getting desired results, they go to the *See* corner and ask questions like: How can I see this differently? How can I see this other person differently? How can I see myself differently? In other words, **Top 20s use curiosity to see things differently.**

> After a week of glaring stares from Maggie, Willow has had enough. She calls Maggie out to the hall and says, "Help me understand something. I'm doing the best I can to make this class interesting for you, but every day I keep getting scowls. What's that about?"
>
> "Oh, Miss Sweeney, I'm not scowling. I'm squinting. My glasses broke and I'm waiting for my new pair to come in. This is my favorite class."
>
> "Well, okay then," says a surprised, yet pleased Willow. "I'm so glad to hear that. Then let's get back into class and keep on going."

Top 20s value curiosity because it allows them to see differently or see more than they originally saw.

## THE NEED TO BE RIGHT VS CURIOSITY

If we are serious about developing potential in ourselves and our students, it is important to be aware of when we have a need to be right.

We have asked thousands of people to describe what they are like or how they behave when they have a need to be right and when they are curious. Some responses include:

| When I Need to be Right, I... | When I Am Curious, I... |
|:---:|:---:|
| Don't listen | Listen |
| Get louder | Am calm |
| Am cocky, smug or arrogant | Am humble |
| Am defensive | Am optimistic |
| Don't ask questions | Ask questions |
| Am closed-minded | Am open-minded |
| Argue my point | Value others' ideas |
| Blame | Search for other possibilities |

Consider what would happen if every teacher, administrator or support staff in our school operated in the need-to-be-right ways. What would be the cost of that collective behavior? Parents would want to take their kids out of our school. Job turnover would be high because staff members would not want to work in such a negative environment.

A major reason why Bottom 80 people are not developing their potential is because their need to be right is manifested in these unproductive behaviors. On the other hand, the potential of Top 20 people is exploding because they are curious. Because curiosity allows them to see more or differently, it gets them totally different results than blame and the need to be right.

**Bottom 80s blame because they need to be right.**

**Top 20s are curious because they need to make a positive difference.**

Parents don't read to their young children books titled *Cocky George, Arrogant George* or *Defensive George*. They read *Curious George* because they recognize the innate value of curiosity and try to promote it in their children.

That raises a challenging question. Which profession on our planet is responsible for maintaining curiosity in kids? Is it lawyers, hair stylists, architects or marine biologists? No, it is our teaching profession. Educators are responsible for fostering children's curiosity. In fact, Top 20 teachers are aware that a fundamental way that a teacher's effectiveness ought to be measured is by how well she keeps curiosity alive in her students.

> "Only the curious will learn
> and only the resolute overcome the obstacles to learning.
> The quest quotient has always excited me more
> than the intelligence quotient."
> —**Eugene S. Wilson**

We do not put curiosity in young children. They come into the world that way. Their *quest quotient* is exceedingly high. A primary responsibility of a Top 20 teacher is to keep it as high as possible. In order to do this, Top 20 teachers are open to seeing ways by which they may be damaging student curiosity. In addition, they need to assist their colleagues and entire teaching profession in becoming aware of ways curiosity is diminished in our classrooms and schools.

## THREE RIGHTS

Have you ever noticed how important it is for people or teachers to be right? Sometimes being right matters more than being effective. When that happens, our need to be right can prevent us from getting the results we desire.

Let's consider three different ways of thinking about being right that are likely to pop up when we're not getting the results we want to be getting.

**R = R** **1. When we think we're right, we're sure we're right.** When the need to be right bubbles up in us and we are convinced that we are right, we don't consider other possibilities or options. This is a Bottom 80 way of thinking because, when we are right in this way, it leads directly to blame.

If we are not getting what is important to us and think we are right, then someone or something else must be wrong and at fault. Since we think we're right, we can just blame them. In blaming them, we give up our power to make a positive difference and stay *stuck in yuck*.

**R = W** **2. When we think we're right, we're aware that we might be wrong but just haven't discovered what we are wrong about yet.** This is a Top 20 way of thinking because it prevents blame and leads to curiosity. Realizing we might be wrong encourages us to keep an open mind, ask questions and listen more. Our curiosity might result in us seeing more or differently and creating a Top 20 experience.

**R = R +** **3. When we think we're right, we are right, but we believe there is still something more that we are not seeing.** This is another Top 20 way of thinking. Top 20s know that there is always something more that they are not seeing. Consequently, even when they know they are right, they maintain curiosity that helps them discover what they did not originally see.

> Tom once handed an Algebra 2 exam to a student who promptly tore it in half, tossed it onto the floor and put his head down on his desk. Tom watched from his desk, realizing that a zero score would give the boy an F for the trimester and a free pass to summer school.
>
> Fortunately, Tom's Top 20 thinking clicked into gear. He approached the student and asked him privately, "What's going on?"
>
> The student sheepishly replied, "My girl friend just dumped me in the hallway ten seconds before the bell rang for this class. I'm a mess. Can I please take this test after school, Mr. Cody?"
>
> Tom agreed and realized that his brief moment of curiosity resulted in a positive experience for both his student and himself. This fifteen seconds of curiosity probably saved both teacher and student hours of agonizing consequences.

What sometimes prevents Bottom 80s from being effective is their fear of being wrong. This keeps them stuck in blame and prevents them from seeing other possibilities. What bothers Top 20 is being *stuck in yuck*. They don't mind being wrong or not knowing everything. They know they always have the curious card to play. It's a winner every time.

## DO YOU SEE OR ARE YOU BLIND

Much of what we cover in this book has to do with seeing: how we see, what we see, old and new ways of seeing. But the fundamental question is: Do we see?

Let's do an experiment. Read the following sentence a couple of times.

> FINISHED FILES ARE THE RESULT OF YEARS
> OF SCIENTIFIC STUDY COMBINED
> WITH THE EXPERIENCE OF MANY YEARS.

Now that you have read the sentence, count the number of F's in the sentence. How many letter F's are in the sentence?

Look again and count the number of F's a second time. Are you coming up with the same number?

We have done this activity hundreds of times with a wide variety of groups. Each time most people will see three F's. A smaller number will see four or five F's. Usually only 20% or less will see six F's (the correct answer) the first time.

What we can learn from this is that we often don't see what is obvious. In this case, we don't see what is black and white. If we often don't see what's obvious, how can we be sure that we see (understand or know) what's not so obvious, like what someone's motive is when he says or does something. Pay attention to the times at school or in your personal life when you hear someone tell you about another person's motives.

Why do we think we can know someone's motive? Because **we think we see things the way they are.** That's rarely the case. Nonetheless, **we can get locked into seeing things a certain way even if that's not the way they really are.**

# PARADIGMS

What we are considering here are paradigms. **Paradigms are the patterned way we see reality.** They are the pictures we have in our head about the way things are. Paradigms form our perspective—the way we see situations, the way we see other people, even the way we see ourselves.

Paradigms are a powerful part of our lives. They can govern our Frame. Because our paradigms are the way we **see,** they influence our emotions (what we **feel**) and our behavior (what we **do**), and, therefore, affect the results (what we **get**). Consequently, changing our paradigm, having a paradigm shift, will cause us to get different results.

When Paul's daughter Megan was three years old, he took her to a basketball game. During the game Megan fell twenty feet through the bleachers and landed head first on the cement floor. As Paul rushed her to the hospital, Megan's head was swelling as if someone was blowing air into a balloon. Paul thought that his young daughter was dead or dying. Although Megan suffered multiple skull fractures from this fall, she eventually gained her full health.

How did this event impact Paul's paradigm of himself as father? A part of every father's paradigm is to protect his children. Because of this incident, protecting his daughter became even a larger part of Paul's paradigm as father.

This paradigm worked well as Megan grew through her grade school years. But once she entered high school, Paul's determination to protect her resulted in her resistance and rebellion. Paul became scared, angry and frustrated by Megan's behavior. After several months he desired relief from this constant problem and said to this wife, "I wish we didn't have her." As painful as that realization was, this was his true feeling. That same week, Paul overheard Megan on the phone telling a friend, "I hate my father." Clearly, neither father nor daughter was getting the results in this relationship that they desired.

At the time Paul was a high school counselor. He realized that the paradigm he had as counselor was different from the paradigm he had as father. The biggest part of his father paradigm was protecting and the biggest part of his counselor paradigm was listening. Paul decided to make a shift from protecting Megan to listening to her. After all, protecting sure wasn't working.

This paradigm shift caused Paul to see Megan, the situation and himself differently. Consequently, he felt and acted differently (more listening) and got different results (eventually a much closer relationship).

## PARADIGMS ARE ALWAYS INCOMPLETE

Although the details of this story are different from your own experiences, your life and Paul's example share some things in common. First, we might hold onto a paradigm even when it isn't working for us, even when

**17**

we are not getting the results that are important to us. One reason we do this is because we think we are right. In fact, we may be. Paul certainly was right in having a paradigm about protecting his daughter. Most every father on earth would agree that that is a correct paradigm.

So why would we change a paradigm if it is correct? **We change if our correct paradigm is not effective in getting the results that are important to us.** We change because we are failing at what we want most. Although Paul's paradigm was *correct*, it was *incomplete*. There was more to the situation than he was seeing, just like the sentence with six F's. Yes, it's true that there are three F's in the sentence. Although that's correct, it's not complete. There are also three more that most people don't see.

It may sound strange to hear that Top 20s are blind, that their paradigms are incomplete and that they don't see reality exactly as it is. What about Bottom 80s? Well, they're blind, too. The difference is that **Top 20s are blind and they know it. Bottom 80s are blind but just don't know it.** They think they see things exactly the way they are.

> "I was looking at life through binoculars, but I was holding them the wrong way. Learning about *seeing* helped me turn them around."
> —Charlie

Knowing that they are blind and that their paradigms are never complete, knowing that they don't see anything (themselves, others or a situation) exactly as it is, Top 20s stay curious and seek additional information. **Top 20s are open to seeing what they don't see.** Consequently, their paradigms are less incomplete than they would have been if they didn't know they were blind.

## PARADIGM SHIFTS: SEEING THINGS DIFFERENTLY

A paradigm shift occurs when we change how we see something. How can we bring this about? How can we see things differently? Following are four ways we can see more or see differently.

**1. Create a Crisis.** The purpose of crisis is to bring about a paradigm shift. The Civil War was a national crisis caused by the belief that human beings could be held as slaves. This was not only an incomplete paradigm but also an incorrect belief.

Crises are very effective in bringing about paradigm shifts. However, the problem with crises is the human pain and suffering involved (such as in the Civil War, the events of 9/11 or Paul and Megan's relationship). While crises often work in getting us to see differently, it will be less painful if we use the other three ways to bring about a shift.

**2. Ask Others How They See It.** Who will see a situation differently than we do? Everyone. No two people see anything exactly alike. By asking someone else how she sees a person or situation, we will expand our paradigm and see it more completely.

It's important to distinguish who we are asking here. We all have that person in our life who will tell us that we are seeing things clearly. Asking that person will not benefit us when we are stuck. We all have that other special person in our life, the one who will challenge the way we are seeing it. That's the person we need to ask if we want to see differently.

**3. Change Roles.** We will automatically change how we see if we change roles. As teachers, we can change roles by asking ourselves how a situation looks through the eyes of our students or their parents or an administrator or a person of a different race or cultural background. Paul looked at his situation through the eyes of a counselor and saw Megan and what he could do very differently. He listened.

> When Tom was coaching basketball, a player who wanted more playing time came to him. Tom asked her what she would do if she were the coach. As she looked at the situation from a coach's point of view, she said she would have her playing about the same amount of time she was already playing. Changing roles got her to see the situation differently.

**4. Say "Maybe."** Have you ever noticed trees growing out of rock? It actually happens. They can't grow out of solid rock but huge trees can grow where there's a crack in a rock.

The same is true for us. If we are hard-headed, if we think we are absolutely right about how we see something, we will never see more or differently. We will stay *stuck in yuck*. What often keeps us stuck are judgments we make. If we think those judgments are correct and complete, they are like solid rock out of which nothing can grow.

Top 20s know that if they put the word "Maybe" before judgments they make, they can create a *crack* in which something else might grow, in which something else is possible. There's a big difference between:

"My teacher hates me" and "Maybe my teacher hates me."

"The next family reunion will be terrible" and "Maybe the next reunion will be terrible."

"Maggie is being rude" and "Maybe Maggie is being rude."

"Megan can't protect herself" and "Maybe Megan can't protect herself."

The power that results from our using the word *maybe* comes from the fact that it might also mean *maybe not.*

## TWO PATHS

In every situation in our life, we can take one of two paths. As we become more and more aware of what each of these paths entails, we will be more able to choose the Top 20 path.

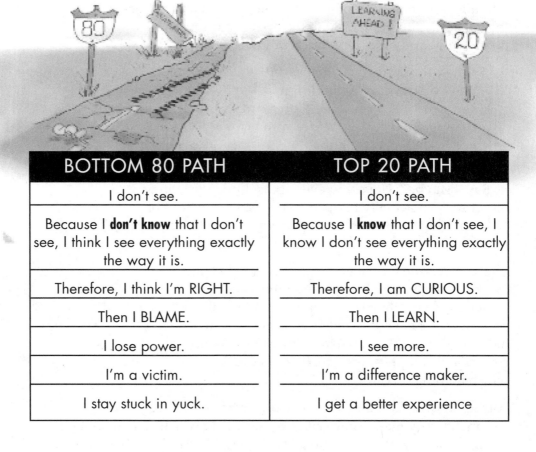

| BOTTOM 80 PATH | TOP 20 PATH |
|---|---|
| I don't see. | I don't see. |
| Because I **don't know** that I don't see, I think I see everything exactly the way it is. | Because I **know** that I don't see, I know I don't see everything exactly the way it is. |
| Therefore, I think I'm RIGHT. | Therefore, I am CURIOUS. |
| Then I BLAME. | Then I LEARN. |
| I lose power. | I see more. |
| I'm a victim. | I'm a difference maker. |
| I stay stuck in yuck. | I get a better experience |

# TIME FOR REFLECTION & ACTION

1. Apply the Frame to a situation in your life where you are not getting the results you would like to be getting:

   A. How are you seeing this situation and the people involved, including yourself?

   B. What are you feeling? Do you have any need to be right?

   C. What are you doing? Are you blaming in any way?

   D. What are the results you are getting?

2. How can you reframe or see this situation differently?

   A. Is it becoming a crisis?

   B. Can you ask someone else how he sees it?

   C. Can you change roles?

   D. Can you put the word *Maybe* before any judgments you have made?

3. What are you doing that is having a positive or negative impact on student curiosity? What is going on in your school that is having a positive or negative impact on student curiosity?

4. What did you become aware of while reading this chapter regarding an action you would like to take? What action would you like to take?

# CHAPTER 3

## TOP 20 TEACHERS

# Are Aware of Their Thinking and Live Above the Line

Miss Robinson felt rushed as she entered her classroom fifteen minutes before her first hour class. Her math department meeting before school had gone longer than expected, and she still had to make copies of tests she would be giving that day. As soon as she put her books and diet soda down on her desk, Cece, a math student, came into the room.

"Good morning, Miss Robinson," said Cece. "May I ask you a question?"

"Can't you see that I'm busy?" responded Miss Robinson, still fumbling with her backpack and looking away from Cece.

"But yesterday you said I should see you before class this morning about my test."

"This isn't a good time. Do you think you're the only student I have to deal with today?"

"Sorry," said Cece as she lowered her head and began to walk out of the room.

"Wait a second, Cece," said Miss Robinson, suddenly aware of how her curt comments had confused Cece. "I'm the one who should be sorry. I just had a few things pile up on me this morning, and I went a bit Below the Line. Would it be possible for us to meet during lunch?"

"Sure, Miss Robinson. Thanks. See you then."

"Have a good morning, Cece. Hope you don't have to deal with any more Below the Line teachers today."

Like Miss Robinson, Top 20 teachers are aware of their thinking. They know when it is Above the Line and working in their best interest and when it is Below the Line and not working in their best interest.

The following illustration depicts what our thinking is like Above the Line and Below the Line.

When we are Above the Line, our thinking is clear and we are aware of what is important. Our TLC is effective. When Below the Line, our thinking is foggy and we lose sight of what is important. Our TLC is ineffective.

**ABOVE THE LINE**
A positive view on life and how I see the world.
My thinking is in my Best Interest.
Energetic moods and emotions:
• Positive attitudes • Hopefulness
• Optimistic • Power to control my life

**BELOW THE LINE**
A negative view on life and how I see the world.
My thinking is <u>not</u> in my Best Interest.
Depressing moods and emotions:
• Negative attitudes • Hopelessness
• Pessimistic • Powerless victim of life

## LIVE AND VISIT

As human beings we can vacillate from Above to Below the Line several times a day. That's normal. However, some people spend most of their time Above the Line. They *live* Above the Line. When in their company, we can feel their positive energy. Do they ever go Below the Line? Of course, but they don't stay there. They only *visit* Below and find ways to bounce back Above the Line as soon as possible.

On the other hand, some people *live* Below. Their thinking is almost always negative. They may *visit* Above the Line but spend a majority of their time Below. It seems as if their life agenda is to complain. When in their company, we may feel our own energy being sucked out of us.

People who live Below the Line may not even be aware of this negative mental habit. They certainly are not aware that they have a choice in the matter.

## LIFE LOOKS DIFFERENT

Being Below the Line is not a bad thing. It's just a human thing. What's important is not to avoid going Below but to be **aware** when we are Below the Line.

Two important reasons indicate the importance of knowing where we are relative to the Line. First, **life looks different whether we are Above or Below the Line.**

When Willow is Above the Line as a mother, she proudly sees her three-year-old son Cooper as a curious kid and loves when he asks her questions: "Mommy, why is the sky blue? Mommy, how do airplanes fly? Mommy, where does milk come from?" But when she is Below the Line, she sees this same son differently. "Cooper, stop asking so many questions. Mommy needs a timeout. Where is your father? Go and ask him."

Teachers sometimes see their students differently. When Above the Line, teachers see their students as energetic, creative, curious or strong willed. When the teachers go Below the Line, those same students are seen as being out of control, disrespectful, apathetic and stubborn.

The same is true about a problem. From Above the Line a problem may look like an opportunity that we are confident we will be able to solve. From Below the Line it may look hopelessly insurmountable. One teacher said, "When I am Above the Line, things that are problems don't even look like problems. When Below the Line, things that aren't problems look like problems."

Because everything in life will look different whether we are Above or Below the Line, it's helpful for us to know where we are.

## DECISIONS BECOME MESSES

The second reason it's important to know where we are on the Line is because **we use our thinking to make decisions.** If our thinking is working in our best interest, we are likely to make good decisions. However, if we are Below the Line and our thinking is not working in our best interest, our decisions will create a mess in our life.

Once Tom became frustrated during a parent conference with an upset mother. She believed her son deserved a better grade in Tom's math class. After all, she said, "He'll be going to Yale some day."

To this seemingly ridiculous statement, Tom sarcastically responded, "He doesn't even bring his notebook to class. You must mean Yale the lock company, not the college."

The next morning Tom's principal wanted to talk to him about the phone call he received from the mother. Tom spent a good part of that day cleaning up the mess he had made from his Below the Line sarcastic response. Even when the apparent mess is cleaned up, Tom still has to deal with his tarnished reputation as the mother repeats his statement to other parents.

Top 20 teachers, knowing when they are Below the Line and their thinking is not working in their best interest, refrain from making important decisions. They wait until they have resurfaced Above the Line and their thinking is clear before they make decisions. Consequently, they avoid many problems that Bottom 80s experience.

Life is precious and we certainly want to have more Above the Line days than Below the Line days. However, if we are not aware of our Line and our ability to govern our own thinking, we can give up perfectly good Above the Line days for all sorts of reasons. Many times we go Below the Line for outside conditions that we cannot control. Too many times, when thinking like a Bottom 80, we choose to go BTL based on silly things like someone taking our parking space or a slouching kid in our class. Top 20s know that this is a choice. Aware of their Line and their power to choose, Top 20s hang on to more Above the Line days than Bottom 80s do.

# INVITATIONS

**Invitations are the conditions that come up in our life that invite us to go Below the Line.** These can arrive several times a day and are sent to us in many forms: an early morning traffic jam, the weather, failure of audio-visual equipment or other technology to function according to our needs, students who don't do their homework, a demanding parent's phone or email message or a plumbing problem in our home. These are invitations to come to a Below the Line party. To these invitations we need to **RSVP.** That means we have a choice. We can decide to go to the Below the Line party or not go to the party. If we choose to attend the party, we are expected to BYON, **Bring Your Own Negativity.** Like a potluck, we share our negativity with others and they share their negativity with us.

**TRUE TALES**

Tom and Paul experienced a major invitation while traveling to Nebraska to do a three-day training for teachers. They arrived in Lincoln on a flight from Minneapolis with several other passengers. After waiting twenty minutes at the carousel for their luggage to arrive, they were informed that no luggage whatsoever had been loaded on this flight.

"Tom," Paul said with a smile, "I think the airline just invited us to come to their Below the Line party. We have to RSVP. Are you interested in going?"

"Don't think so," said Tom matter-of-factly, while standing in line at the counter. "I'm fifty-six years old. I can't afford to be giving days away at this point in my life."

Although Tom and Paul rejected the invitation to the Below the Line party, the other passengers in front of them in line decided to go Below. Each had to meet with Brent, a young man who worked for the airlines and was trying to help recover everyone's luggage. As each of these passengers came to Brent's counter, they brought their negativity and dumped it on him.

When Tom finally made it to Brent, he asked with tongue in cheek, "So, Brent, how has your day been so far?"

Brent chuckled and indicated that it hadn't been going so well.

"How can we help you?" asked Paul.

"Well," said Brent, "just describe your luggage and tell me where you are staying tonight."

After giving Brent the information, Paul and Tom thanked Brent for his kind service in trying to recover their luggage.

"The next flight from Minneapolis will be coming in at 11:00 tonight," said Brent. "Everyone's luggage will be on that plane but yours will be the first delivered."

The point of this story is that when we are aware of our Line and take care of our inside first, we sometimes can have a positive influence on outside conditions. Likewise, when we accept invitations to Below the Line parties, we really are likely to make matters worse. After all, decisions Below the Line usually turn out to be a mess.

## CONDITIONS OR EXPERIENCE

Top 20s realize the difference between conditions and experience. Although they do not control outside conditions (luggage that doesn't arrive, students with incomplete homework, changes in class schedules), they are able to control the inside experience. For Top 20s, **conditions do not determine the experience.** Their thinking determines the experience. Bottom 80s, on the other hand, believe that outside conditions determine their experience. They blame what's *out there* for what's going on *in here*. In doing so, they give up their power to make a positive difference in their life.

We are all free to operate this way. It's just that when we do so we give away a lot of happy days or experiences.

# INDICATORS

How do we know when we are Below the Line? How do we know when our thinking is not working in our best interest? We know by paying attention to our Indicators. **Indicators are the feelings we have or the behaviors we exhibit when we are Below the Line.**

There are countless Indicators, but the following list suggests some common ones.

Feelings: frustrated, angry, stressed, irritated, tired, depressed

Behaviors: withdrawing (getting quiet), being sarcastic or aggressive (getting loud, arguing, needing to be right), blaming, procrastinating, complaining

People are different and not everyone shares the same Indicators. What is helpful is to be aware of our own Indicators and those of our colleagues or family members. If as teachers we are not aware of our own Indicators, our students probably are.

# SUBMARINE

We will all have moments Below the Line. That's normal. **Submarine is a metaphor for handling our BTL experiences with grace and dignity.** Being in a Submarine allows us to have a safer experience. We have ample air, are protected from outside sharks and outside sharks are protected from us. Similarly, when we go Below the Line, we want to do it in a fashion that is safe for others and ourselves.

As a basketball coach, Paul once went to practice Below the Line. Two of his dominant Indicators of being Below the Line are the negative tone of his voice and his need to be right. Imagine being the high school players on his team who had to put up with his tone and need to be right during two hours of practice. His negativity would have spilled onto them. They would have shared it with each other in the locker room after practice by complaining about their coach. Then they would have complained about him during dinner with their family, thus creating a Below the Line party.

However, none of this happened because, although he was below the line, Paul went to practice in a Submarine. When his team came into the gym, he said, "Look, Coach B is Below the Line today. This has nothing to do with you. Please don't take anything I say personally."

Throughout practice they got his negative tone and need to be right but did not take those on. Consequently, he was not a topic of conversation in the locker room or at the dinner table. By using a Submarine and telling the kids about his being BTL, his negativity was contained and no Below the Line party resulted.

Let's be clear. The fact that Paul told his team that he was Below the Line does not give him permission to abuse his players by yelling and screaming at them. But by going Below the Line in a Submarine, we are able to be more graceful with our negativity.

Let's assume that Paul had not told his team that he was Below the Line. What would likely be going through the mind of his players while he explains an out-of-bounds play during practice? Some of his players might be thinking: "Why is coach mad at me? Did I make a mistake in the last game? Is he not going to play me anymore?" Because they are being distracted by these thoughts, they are not focusing on how to run the out-of-bounds play. When they run it improperly in practice, the coach is likely to come down on them for messing up the play. As a result, more negativity gets sent back and forth between coach and players.

Obviously, this same dynamic can occur in the classroom. The negativity we bring to the classroom when we are Below the Line can get dumped on our students. As it affects their experience and learning, it can draw out negativity from them. Top 20 teachers prevent this from happening by being aware when they are Below the Line and using a Submarine to handle their negativity more effectively.

What if the issue that invites us to go Below the Line *is* our students or players? Willow handles this by saying, "I'm Below the Line this morning. There is something we need to talk about. However, because I'm Below the Line right now, this isn't a good time. I'll share it with you when my thinking is clearer."

Tom handles this situation in a different manner. He has an Above and Below the Line chart in his classroom with a picture of himself pinned to it. When he's BTL, he asks one of his students to pin his picture Below the Line and then says, "I corrected your quizzes. I'm choosing to go Below the Line. I need about 27 seconds."

A student timing him will say, "Go, Mr. Cody."

Then he lets it out, "Many of you did poorly on this test, but none of you came in for extra help or even asked questions in class. You're wasting your time and mine. Are all of you astronauts planning a trip to Mars and too busy to come in for help? This has got to change or…"

"Time's up, Mr. Cody," says the student watching the clock who then takes Tom's picture and pins it Above the Line.

"OK, I'm back," he says with a smile. "Let's get to today's lesson."

Tom's method only works because he had previously shared the Submarine concept with his students in order to make it part of the classroom culture. By handling his Below the Line moments with his students directly, emotionally and humorously, Tom vents his feelings and gets his point across without damaging his students with lasting negativity. After all, what do students who have just done poorly on a test need? Certainly not a teacher who is stuck Below the Line. Bottom 80 teachers can get stuck Below the Line for the whole period…or for the morning…or for the week… or until retirement.

## TRAMPOLINES

Like Tom, Top 20 teachers have Below the Line experiences, but they don't stay there for long periods of time. They use Trampolines to resurface their Submarine ATL. **Trampolines are means by which we can get our thinking working once again in our best interest.** Trampolines help us regain clarity in our thinking and focus on what is most important. As such, we are less likely to give away our day or make a decision that creates a mess.

Top 20 teachers have unique Trampolines that work for them. Some of these might include:

| | | |
|---|---|---|
| Exercising | Laughing | Napping |
| Talking to a friend | Praying or meditating | Taking quiet time |
| Listening to music | Enjoying a hobby | Playing with pets |

Teachers can only use these Trampolines to keep themselves emotionally healthy when time allows. We can't say to a third period class, "Ms. Sweeney needs to get Above the Line. I'm going to go for a jog and then take a nap. Be good and I'll be back in an hour!" So sometimes we need to find a Trampoline we can utilize when we don't have time for our favorite activities.

**Gaining perspective** can be this kind of Trampoline. Willow gains perspective by remembering a special friend who recently died from cancer. Willow trampolines Above by realizing that life is precious and not worth wasting time complaining about silly things. Tom carries a small rock in his pocket from Homer, Alaska. It reminds him of a brilliant sunrise he experienced there while vacationing with his son. Paul recalls special times with his grandchildren. By simply thinking of them, Paul is filled with joy. Gaining perspective is an effective Trampoline because it connects us to what is truly important in our life.

The same is true for **gratitude**. Being grateful elevates us from *poor me* thinking and complaining. Yes, we may be encountering difficulties in our life but gratitude activates an awareness of all that is positive in our lives as well.

**Random acts of kindness** can also activate positive energy in us. Shoveling a neighbor's sidewalk, carrying a bag of groceries for a senior citizen, welcoming a new teacher on our staff or sending a positive message to the parents of a struggling student can stir in us the realization that we can make a difference in someone's life.

We have met countless Top 20 teachers throughout the country. Not only do they make a difference in their own lives by being aware of their Line and Indicators, knowing that they have a choice when they receive Invitations, and using Submarines and Trampolines, but they also make a difference in their students' lives by passing this awareness on to them. As such, Top 20 teachers give their students hope by awakening in them their own power to make a positive difference in their lives.

# BETH: AN INSPIRATION

We have talked about using awareness of the Line for dealing with traffic jams, problems with technology, kids without homework or angry calls from parents, but what about more serious circumstances that come up in our lives?

Not only do students learn from their teachers but also teachers learn from their students. Few students have taught us as much as Beth has.

While a freshman in high school, Beth took a Top 20 class where she learned about the concepts presented in this book. One day Beth's father was diagnosed with a life threatening condition. Within weeks, he died from this illness. Beth missed several days of school for the wake and funeral and dealing with this tremendous loss. Upon her return to class, she shared with her teachers that she wanted to talk about the Line.

"I have been given a green light to live Below the Line," Beth said. "I could do just about anything and people would understand. They'd cut me slack if I argued with my mother, was nasty to my brother and never did any homework. But I'm not going to do that. That would dishonor my father's life. I am going to grieve his loss from Above the Line."

This is a fourteen-year-old kid who, during the most difficult experience of her young life, discovered a power in her to choose the experience she was going to have. Was Beth a victim of outside circumstances? Absolutely. Had she been sent an Invitation to go Below the Line? Certainly one of the biggest Invitations a young person can get. But Beth knew she had the power not to live this experience of her life as a victim. She knew she had the power to decline the Invitation.

Although she was experiencing tremendous loss, she knew she could grieve the loss of her father from Above the Line. As such, she did what she needed to do to take care of herself and her family. She even brought cupcakes to school to share with her friends at lunch. During that lunch, she and her friends talked about and celebrated their fathers. She then asked her friends to go home and hug their dads.

At the most difficult moment in her life, Beth was aware of her Line. In doing so, she maintained her power of choice and created the best experience possible for herself and others.

## TWO CHOICES

In any situation in life, we have two choices. We can respond as a Bottom 80 or a Top 20.

Bottom 80s wait for outside conditions to improve,
then their inside experience is better.

Top 20s take care of their inside first,
then their outside conditions get better.

Regardless of the circumstances in our life, we can be a Bottom 80, see ourselves as a victim and blame others, or be a Top 20, maintain our responsibility to keep our power and choose to make a positive difference in our life.

Jeanne Schwabacher, a Top 20 teacher at Jackson Elementary School in St. Paul, Minnesota, has taught her largely immigrant sixth grade students Above and Below the Line. "My students," says Jeanne, "are no longer *characters* in someone else's story. They are *authors* of their own." As authors, these young students are passing on their power to their younger brothers and sisters.

**All students need Top 20 teachers
so they can become authors of their own lives.**

# TIME FOR REFLECTION & ACTION

1. Identify a decision you made while you were Below the Line. What was the outcome of that decision? What might you have done differently if you had been aware that you were Below the Line and that your thinking was not working in your best interest?

2. What are your:

A. Invitations?
B. Indicators?
C. Trampolines?

3. How might you use the Submarine concept to handle Below the Line moments with more grace and dignity?

4. What did you become aware of while reading this chapter regarding an action you would like to take? What action would you like to take?

# CHAPTER 4

## TOP 20 TEACHERS

# Create Safety and a Positive Work Environment

It was Bill's first day of teaching at Mehlville Middle School. As his students left his room for lunch, Bill saw Mr. Gonzales, who taught in a nearby classroom, waiting at the door.

"Bill, would you like to join me for lunch?" invited Mr. Gonzales.

"Sure would," said Bill. "Thanks for asking."

On their way to lunch, Mr. Gonzales smiled at the students in the hallway and picked up and discarded a paper cup that someone had dropped on the floor. He asked Bill how his first morning had gone and expressed how much he enjoyed the enthusiasm of his new students. Upon entering the faculty lounge, they sat at a table with four other teachers.

"Summer wasn't long enough," commented Sharon, a language arts teacher.

"And now nine months of this," added Robert.

"My schedule gets worse every year," complained Maria.

"Mr. Cronin has his favorites, but I'm not one of them," said Marty about the assistant principal responsible for scheduling.

"On a positive note, have you heard about Jimmy Owens?" asked Mr. Gonzales, referring to one of the eighth grade students. "He received his Boy Scout Eagle Award by completing a project that provided transportation for senior citizens."

Although most of our day as teachers is spent with students in a classroom, we also interact with other adults. Teaching requires a great deal of energy. The rapid pace of a school day does not allow for many opportunities to relax and reenergize. Besides planning classes, teaching lessons and correcting papers, we also contribute to the culture and the climate in our building.

The atmosphere that is created by what we exchange with each other can either drain us before the first bell rings in the morning or sustain us through the challenges of a school year. **Top 20 teachers like Mr. Gonzales create a healthy work environment through the positive energy they communicate.**

## SAFETY: THE ESSENCE OF A POSITIVE WORK ENVIRONMENT

The culture and climate in which we work has a major impact on our energy and the amount of potential we develop as we work together.

Paul recently flew across the country to work with a consulting group. After a long day of travel, he spent two full days with three other people planning, brainstorming and creating a 32-hour training program for mentally handicapped adults.

On his return flight, he wondered why he wasn't feeling exhausted. In fact, he felt so relaxed and energized that it was as if he had been on vacation for three days. What he realized was that all the energy that had been expressed by this work group had been totally positive. The collective positive energy of the group not only accomplished a great deal of work but also actually refreshed the minds, bodies and spirits of four people.

What was really being created during these very busy days? What really caused Paul to feel refreshed and not exhausted? Safety. Because the people he was working with created an environment in which Paul experienced physical, emotional and spiritual safety, he was more renewed than spent.

The positive energy that creates safety allows a person the freedom to be herself. Freedom to be self is the antidote to stress. Stress is the inner call for energy to deal with the tension resulting from a person's need to protect herself. Stress results when we are not safe, when we are experiencing a real or perceived threat.

> Positive Energy  ➤ Safety  ➤ Freedom to be self ➤ Peace
> Negative Energy ➤ Threat ➤ Need to protect    ➤ Stress

Whereas a negative environment drains us of our energy, a positive environment restores our energy.

**Top 20 teachers know they are responsible not only for what goes on in the classroom but also for what goes on in the culture of their school.** In a variety of ways, they do things that create safety and a positive work environment. Most important of these is their daily focus on doing Job #1.

# JOB #1: HELP OTHERS SUCCEED

Teachers are hired to teach, but their primary job should be to help others succeed. We call this Job #1. Although it's not written on a job description, **a Top 20 teacher knows that her chief task each day is to help other people succeed.** She does what she can to help students learn, help a colleague teach, help a principal lead, help a parent parent or help an attendance clerk, secretary or maintenance person do their work.

Likewise, administrators are hired to administrate, but their Job #1 is to help their staff, faculty and students succeed. Secretaries are hired to do secretarial work, but their Job #1 is to help the members of their school community succeed. Coaches are hired to coach, but their Job #1 is to help their players, parents and others in the school succeed.

Although they are not hired help, this same Job #1 ought to be expected of students. Students come to school to learn, but their first job is to help others succeed. They are to do what they can to help teachers and administrators succeed, to help the secretarial staff and the maintenance crew succeed and, maybe most importantly, to help classmates succeed.

If this were everyone's Job #1, the school community would function as a team. **A team is a group of people who help each other succeed in order to achieve important goals.** If Job #1 were the common practice of teachers, coaches, administrators, support staff, students and parents, then everyone in a school would know that everyone else is helping him succeed. In such a positive culture, potential would explode.

Isn't it easy to be cynical about this idea of Job #1? Isn't it way too idealistic to think that everyone is going to help everyone else succeed? It certainly is idealistic. However, the problem with Job #1 isn't that it's idealistic, it's that it's not even expected.

If it were expected, would everyone operate this way all the time? Of course not. But most people do what's expected most of the time. Our schools wouldn't become perfect, but they would become better. Not until

Job #1 is expected, not until students and adults who come together every day expect to be a team, not until they help each other succeed will schools become places where potential really explodes.

A team is capable of accomplishing far more than a collection of individuals. Job #1 creates the expectation that we are to operate as a team. Every effort that creates team also creates safety and a positive environment.

**A safe and positive culture**
**is the environment in which potential explodes.**

Furthermore, what students would learn from this experience would help them be successful in everything they do after they leave school. Learning how to help other people succeed would help them succeed in their future families, work places and communities. We would be developing a generation whose thinking shifts from a **ME** mentality to a **WE** mentality. The safety and positive energy that would flow from this would explode the potential not only in our schools but also in our country.

Job #1 does not mean that we run around the school doing other people's work. What it does mean is that we have a frame of mind that is looking out for whatever others need to succeed or have a positive experience. It means that, once we become aware of what they may need, we do what we can to respond to that need. It's expected to help when we can help.

> "Do what you can, with what you have, where you are."
> **Theodore Roosevelt**

People who work in a school can create safety and a positive work environment and address Job #1 in countless ways. Top 20 teachers are particularly aware that three ways of achieving safety and a positive work experience are by communicating "You matter," honoring the absent and owning the problem.

# 1. COMMUNICATE "YOU MATTER"

Paul had a scheduled appointment with a school administrator. Finding that the administrator was not in her office, he knocked on the adjacent office door. Emily turned away from her computer and said, "Good morning. Can I help you?"

"I have an appointment with Dr. Reilly," Paul responded, "but she's not in her office."

"Let's see if we can find her. Come with me," said Emily. She introduced herself and led Paul to the main office where she inquired about Dr. Reilly's whereabouts. Learning that Dr. Reilly would return shortly, Emily led Paul to a waiting area and offered to get him something to drink.

The most powerful thing that can happen in human interaction took place in the few moments Emily spent with Paul. She communicated You Matter. It would have been understandable that when Paul knocked on Emily's office door looking for Dr. Reilly, that Emily would have responded by saying, "I'm sorry, but I don't know where she is right now." That would have been cordial and polite, but it would not have communicated You Matter.

There are certainly many ways of communicating "You matter." In the story at the beginning of this chapter, Mr. Gonzales communicated "You matter" by inviting the new teacher to lunch. Top 20 teachers do this by seeking what is in the best interest of their students, listening to understand their students' needs, struggles or point of view, and valuing the different opinions, perspectives or life experiences of their students and colleagues.

## 2. HONORING THE ABSENT

If we are serious about developing the potential within our students and faculty, then we have to be serious about building and maintaining trust. For a group's potential to explode, trust is a critical and essential requirement. If trust is low, there is no safety. If there is no safety, potential cannot develop fully.

A major means by which trust is established within a group is by **honoring the absent.** When we speak well of people who are not present, we are actually building trust with those who are present. Likewise, if we speak ill of people who are not present, **if we dishonor the absent, we violate trust with people who are present.** The obvious reason for this is that people who hear us dishonoring the absent will assume that we will dishonor them when they are not present.

Imagine that your life is like a lake. If we are around people who are continually dishonoring the absent and complaining about others, it's as if our lake is getting polluted. If this is happening, it's because we have put a *Dump Here* sign near

our lake. In other words, we are saying or doing things that are inviting others to feel comfortable dumping negativity around us.

A way to change the sign to *No Dumping Here* is to become a **problem solver** rather than a **problem namer.** For example, if a teacher says, "That new teacher in our department isn't working out. He doesn't have a clue how to develop a lesson or manage a class. He won't be here long." This teacher is not trying to problem solve but merely to problem name.

Problem namers look for allies; they want someone to agree with them. Problem solvers look for solutions; they want to make things better.

If we listen to problem namers, over time they will dump more and more garbage into our lake. To avoid our lake from getting polluted, we can respond as a problem solver. To the example of the teacher's dishonoring complaint above, a Top 20 teacher might say, "You seem concerned about the new teacher. Let's bring your concerns to him and see if we can be supportive."

To this the complaining teacher might respond with an excuse, something like, "You know, I have a dentist appointment. I'll see you later." But the next time this teacher wants to dishonor the absent, she's not going back to the Top 20 teacher. Top 20 teachers put *No Dumping Here* signs next to their lake. As a result, their lakes stay clean and the dishonoring teacher will have to find someone else next time she wants to dump.

Because Top 20 teachers are problem solvers, they tend not to attract problem namers into their lives. Besides doing what they can to keep their own lake clean, they are helping to keep their school's lake clean as well.

Have you ever worked at a school where some teachers won't go into the faculty lounge? That's because the faculty lounge has become a polluted lake. That's what's happening between the four teachers with whom Bill and Mr. Gonzales sat down to have lunch. Each one was a problem namer.

By honoring or dishonoring the absent, people in every workplace decide whether or not a person's name is sacred. If we dishonor the absent, if we complain about another teacher or administrator, if we badmouth a student or parent, then we are deciding that someone's name is not sacred. But guess what? As soon as we decide that one person's name is not sacred, we are really deciding that no one's name is sacred. Not any teacher's or administrator's, not any student's or parent's, not even our own.

# NAME IS SACRED

What can we do to build trust in our workplace and eliminate dishonoring the absent? Top 20 teachers practice the **2-Out-of-3 Rule**. The 2-Out-of-3 Rule identifies three behaviors:

1. We can say someone else's name.

2. We can say something negative about that person.

3. We can say it to someone else.

If we do all three of these, we are dishonoring the absent. However, if we do only two, we are not dishonoring the absent.

For example, we can do #1 and #2: We can say, "I'm really frustrated with Bill because he never shares his opinion at any of our department meetings." We just can't say it to someone else. We can take this frustration and tell it to the nearest tree or family pet. We just can't say it to another person who can spread this negativity.

We can do #1 and #3: We can say, "Mr. Gonzales, I think it's wonderful the way Bill listens to everyone's opinions during our department meetings." We just can't say something negative. It's fine to use someone's name in the company of another person as long as it's used in a positive way.

We can do #2 and #3: We can say, "Mr. Gonzales, I'm really feeling frustrated today." We just can't use someone's name or say it in a way that identifies the person: "I'm really frustrated by the new teacher in our department." We can vent our feelings to others without dishonoring the absent in the process.

Although Top 20 teachers are acutely aware of the need to build and maintain trust within the faculty and school culture and, as a result, frequently practice the 2-Out-of-3 Rule, at times they need to do all three. At times they need to say someone else's name, say something negative about that person and say it to someone else.

Imagine that Billy Henderson is your fourth grade student and you are talking to other teachers who have Billy in class.

Example 1: Dishonoring the Absent

"Billy Henderson hasn't done a stitch of homework all week. He just doesn't care about school. And his parents didn't even come to parent conferences. No wonder Billy doesn't care about school."

A comment such as this may be coming out of a teacher's genuine frustration and desire for Billy to do well in school. The teacher may be unaware that he is just problem naming. Nonetheless, he is dishonoring the Henderson name. A Top 20 teacher would handle this differently.

Example 2: Honoring the Absent

"I'm concerned about Billy Henderson. He hasn't done any homework all week. And I noticed that his parents didn't attend parent conferences. Is there anything we can do to help Billy and his parents be more connected with school?"

This Top 20 teacher is (#1) using Billy's name, (#2) talking about something negative and (#3) saying it to someone else. However, she is problem solving, not problem naming. She is not looking for allies to agree with her; she is looking for solutions that might help Billy and his parents.

Expressing a concern in this way may result in Billy and his parents having a more positive school experience. However, even if it doesn't, this teacher is building trust among her colleagues by honoring the absent and respecting the Henderson name. She is communicating You Matter to the Henderson family and everyone else she works with and teaches. As a problem solver and trust builder, she is doing Job #1 and helping others succeed.

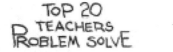

TOP 20 TEACHERS PROBLEM SOLVE        BOTTOM 80 TEACHERS PROBLEM NAME

The habit of dishonoring the absent is common in our culture. In fact, most American humor is now the result of dishonoring the absent. Some political figure, movie star, athlete or celebrity who is not present is made fun of by the late night talk show host and we all laugh. That's the equivalent of putting a *Dump Here* sign in front of our national lake.

Political figures and other leaders often swim in these polluted waters themselves. They dishonor members of the opposite party whenever that opportunity arises.

We may not be able to do much to influence the dishonoring that goes on within our national culture, but we certainly can influence what goes on in our classrooms, faculty lounges and schools. We can create safety and a positive work and learning environment by honoring the absent.

Maybe by honoring the absent at this level and holding peoples' names as sacred we can discourage the dishonoring humor and discourse in the public arena that pollutes our culture and prevents our potential as a people from exploding in wonderful ways. Although our students and schools are influenced by our larger social culture, Top 20 teachers know that influence also goes in the other direction. By honoring our students and adults in our schools, we can assist the clean-up process in our national lake.

# 3. SEE THE PROBLEM, OWN THE PROBLEM

What do we do when we become aware of problems that are not directly attributable to ourselves? Bottom 80s seldom take responsibility for problems, especially when they are not their own. Rather, they commonly respond by doing nothing, complaining or blaming someone else.

A stated service value of people employed at the Ritz-Carlton Hotel Company is: **I own and immediately resolve guest problems.** A story is told about a guest who, while checking into a Ritz-Carlton Hotel late one evening, asked the clerk if room service was still available. It would have been reasonable had the clerk informed the guest that room service was no longer available. Since it was quite late, the guest would have understood that and, although hungry, would not have felt that he had been poorly served. However, that is not the value for employees at the Ritz-Carlton. Consequently, after escorting the guest to his room, the clerk went to the kitchen, made a sandwich and brought it to the guest.

In this culture, people who see the problem own the problem. They take responsibility to do whatever they can to solve the problem. That's a Top 20 response. It's the way Mr. Gonzales responded when he picked up the paper cup in the hallway. It's the way Emily responded when Paul came to her school for a meeting. It's a powerful way of being a team and communicating You Matter.

Consider what would happen on a football team if the running back fumbled the ball. As soon as his teammates saw the loose ball, they would immediately dive on the ball and try to recover the fumble. They would see the problem and own the problem.

In the workplace that is seldom the response. Bottom 80s are likely to respond to someone else's mistake by doing nothing ("It's someone else's job.") or telling someone else about it. Imagine a football player after seeing a teammate fumble the ball saying to another player, "Did you see what the running back just did? He fumbled the ball."

On a team those would be ridiculous responses. If we want to tap into the power of a team, we need to respond differently. When we see the problem and own the problem, when we help a student or colleague who have fumbled, we are communicating to her You Matter and doing Job #1.

## POTENTIAL DEVELOPS WHEN SOMEONE GETS INSIDE OUR WORLD

Think of a seed whose potential never develops because it remains unplanted. If it is planted, what really happens to develop its potential? The potential of the seed only begins to develop when rain from the clouds, energy from the sun and nutrients from the soil enter the seed. The water, sun and nutrients are not the seed, but they are necessary if the seed is going to grow. This only happens when those items that are different from the seed actually get inside the seed.

The same is true for our students and ourselves. We can only grow and develop if we are in a relationship in which someone else enters our world. Unlike a seed that has no choice as to what comes into it, human beings young and old do have that choice. They choose who they allow into their lives. That choice is largely based on who is viewed as being safe. If someone is safe, students open the door to their lives and let that person enter. If someone is not viewed as safe, the door stays shut.

Many of our students come to our schools each day from having lived with a fear or threat in their homes, communities and peer relationships. Many of our students experience similar fear and threat within our schools. They are unable to learn. These fears and threats can be physical, emotional or psychological. To various degrees all human beings experiences fears and threats that impact their work or learning. If these are significant for students or adults, they will not be able to enjoy successful work or learning experiences.

Top 20 teachers understand the many fears and threats that are brought into our classrooms, hallways and school culture that make learning and the full development of potential difficult. They also understand the fundamental need for safety in our schools in order to counter these anxieties. Efforts to keep physical violence out of schools have been well publicized. Top 20 teachers, realizing that we need to be just as diligent in maintaining emotional safety in schools, consciously create a Top 20 culture.

# TIME FOR REFLECTION & ACTION

1. How safe is the environment in which you work? How free are students and adults to be themselves?

2. How aware or effective are you in:

   A. Accomplishing Job #1?

   B. Communicating You Matter?

   C. Honoring the Absent?

   D. Seeing the Problem and Owning the Problem?

3. What did you become aware of while reading this chapter regarding an action you would like to take? What action would you like to take?

# CHAPTER 5

## TOP 20 TEACHERS

# Know the Power of Messages and Beliefs

Although blind and deaf, Helen Keller became a world-famous speaker, authored twelve books and was an activist for social equality. She campaigned for women's suffrage, workers' rights and people with disabilities. She learned Braille to read English, French, German, Greek, and Latin. Graduating from Radcliffe magna cum laude, she became the first deaf and blind person to earn a Bachelor of Arts degree. She devoted much of her life raising funds for the American Foundation for the Blind and founded a research institute for vision, health and nutrition.

Helen was awarded the Presidential Medal of Freedom, one of the United States' highest civilian honors, and was elected to the Women's Hall of Fame at the New York World's Fair. She is listed in Gallup's Most Widely Admired People of the 20th Century, honored on the state quarter of Alabama, has a hospital dedicated to her and a street named after her in Getafe, Spain. She met every president from Grover Cleveland to Lyndon B. Johnson and was friends with many famous figures, including Alexander Graham Bell, Charlie Chaplin and Mark Twain. Her life story was made into a play and film called *The Miracle Worker.*

The spirit and contributions of Helen Keller came to the world because of a teacher's belief. Ann Sullivan's belief that her young student could learn was the force that broke through Helen's isolation allowing her to communicate and become one of the greatest contributors of the 20th century.

## BELIEF ACTIVATES POTENTIAL

Think of a farmer who has sacks of corn seed in his barn. Why would that farmer spend countless hours taking that seed and planting it in his fields? He believes there is potential in each seed to become a stalk and yield ears of corn. Without that belief, the seeds would never get planted and their potential would remain dormant.

**The most powerful thing that Top 20 teachers bring into a classroom is a belief in the potential of their students, their belief that their students can learn.** Top 20 teachers realize that **beliefs activate potential.**

The reason for this is the Frame. Top 20 teachers know that what they are getting is greatly influenced by how they see. However, they also know that beliefs influence how they see. Because of their beliefs, they see things in a certain way.

- If we believe a student doesn't care about school or learning, we will see her based on that belief.
- If we believe a child is disrespectful, we will see him based on that belief.
- If we believe that a student is curious and wants to learn, we will see her based on that belief.

Beliefs come in two varieties: potential activating beliefs and potential limiting beliefs. Just as a farmer's belief in the potential of corn seed results in a rich fall harvest, a farmer's belief that there is no potential in corn seed would result in no harvest at all. Similarly, Ann Sullivan's belief that Helen Keller could learn resulted in her student's incredible accomplishments. If Ann had believed that Helen's learning was hopeless, her student's potential would have remained dormant.

## MESSAGES INFLUENCE BELIEFS

Beliefs don't just pop into our head. They are formed. One of the major causes for the formation of beliefs is messages that we have received. Messages come from a variety of sources: parents, teachers, peers, the media and even ourselves. They remain outside messages until we accept them as true. At the moment that we accept a message, it becomes our belief. In a real sense, therefore, what we *get* out of life may have a lot to do with messages that we have received.

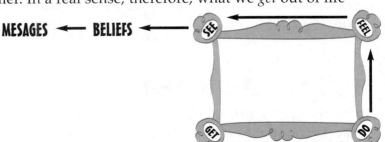

Let's consider the example of a woman who attended our training.

> While Mary was in college, a professor said to her in a condescending way, "Mary, you should go back to high school and learn how to write." Although she did not actually return to high school, Mary accepted this message and it became a powerful belief.
>
> A gifted and intelligent woman, Mary eventually became an administrator for a large school district. People on her staff found her writing to be clear, concise and creative. However, because Mary believed she was a poor writer, whenever she had to submit a written report or proposal, she would dread doing it and procrastinate.

Why was it so painfully difficult for her to complete such projects? The belief that she was not a good enough writer governed the experience Mary had for several years. Her struggle stemmed solely from a belief that had been formed by a simple message sent by a college professor.

Once Mary became aware of how her Frame was influenced by messages and beliefs, she was able to minimize the negative impact of a single message and self-limiting belief. Writing was no longer a painful chore that needed to be avoided but a means of expressing her talent and potential.

> While in fifth grade, Paul was sick and missed a week of school. When he began to feel better, Paul's parents told him that he could return to school but couldn't play in the basketball game that night. Paul informed his fifth grade teacher, who was also his basketball coach, that he could be in school but couldn't play in the game. His teacher responded by saying to Paul, "You have a yellow streak down your back. You're afraid to play in the game."
>
> Although Paul didn't respond to his teacher's message by saying anything verbally, he thought, "No, I'm not afraid to play basketball. I'd love to play. I'm not playing because my parents won't allow it."

Because Paul never accepted his teacher's message, it never became a belief.

## CORE MESSAGES

Each human being is wired with three Core messages that are intended to guide and direct her life towards fulfillment. These Core messages have to do with Identity, Worth and Purpose.

**Identity:** At her Core each person is a unique identity. This identity is the True Self or the essence of each individual. Like Helen Keller, each student has a unique identity unlike any other person on earth.

**Worth:** At her Core each person has a sense of worth. The value of a person at her Core comes from simply being. It is not connected to *doing* or resulting from achievements or accomplishments. Helen's essential worth came from her being a person, not from the many wonderful things she accomplished throughout her life.

**Purpose:** At her Core each person's purpose is to be her True Self. She can admire someone else and appreciate his qualities, but her purpose is not to be someone else. Helen's purpose in life was not to be Mark Twain or Eleanor Roosevelt. Her purpose was to be her own True Self, to develop the potential that is Helen Keller.

A Jewish rabbi named Zushye is known to have said, "When I get to the after life, I will not be asked, 'Why were you not Moses?' I will be asked, 'Why were you not Zushye?'" Like Zushye, our purpose in life is to be our True Self with our unique identity and potential.

## CIRCUMFERENCE MESSAGES

When we are born, we find ourselves on the Circumference or in the Land of Other People. While there we begin to receive other messages. Messages on the Circumference tend to take the form of OPOs, OPEs and OPAs.

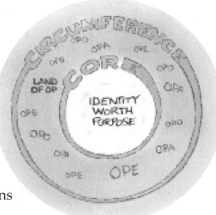

> OPOs = Other Peoples' Opinions
> OPEs = Other Peoples' Expectations
> OPAs = Other Peoples' Agendas

In a variety of ways, OPOs, OPEs and OPAs provide messages that tell us how we are to think, feel and behave, what we are to say, wear, drive, drink, and read, who we are to date, marry, or vote for, where we are to go to school, work, live or vacation, and so on.

As we listen more and more to the OPOs, OPEs and OPAs that bombard us from the Land of Other People, we begin to believe that our purpose in life is to Please Other People. This becomes obvious because we recognize that when we please other people they give us things we like: toys, treats, good grades, invitations, jobs, promotions, money and compliments.

We also notice that when we don't please others they give us things: criticism, poor grades, the *look*, punishment, demotions and pink slips. As we focus our attention on OPOs, OPEs and OPAs and direct our energy towards Pleasing Other People, we can forget about our Core messages. That's the danger we can encounter while we live in the Land of Other People, a danger that strips us of our True Self without our even being aware that it's happening.

But there can also be a blessing in the Land of Other People. Sometimes we meet other people whose Opinions, Expectations or Agendas encourage us to be our True Self. In fact, sometimes we can have experiences on the Circumference that actually remind us of our true identity, worth and purpose.

It is a responsibility of Top 20 teachers
  • to have opinions that recognize the true identity and worth of a child,
  • to have expectations that draw forth the unique potential of a child,
  • to have an agenda that empowers a child to become his True Self.

Ann Sullivan did not transform Helen into someone she was not. Rather, she awakened the true Helen and activated the spirit, talents and potential that had always been in this young girl.

# THE LAWS OF BELIEF

Our lives are greatly influenced by three Laws of Belief.

**1. The Law of Beliefs: The basic Law of Beliefs states that whatever we believe is real for us.** If we believe something to be true, we are likely to have experiences that are in line with that belief. If we believe we will succeed, we are more likely to succeed. If we believe we will fail, we are more likely to fail.

> *"To accomplish great things, we must not only act, but also dream, not only plan, but also dream."*
> **Anatole France**

Have you ever noticed how athletic teams after championship games or seasons give credit to believing? "We believed we could do it." This is not a coincidence. Believing is the beginning of achieving. The reason for this is that beliefs impact how we see. They become the lens through which we see reality. As such, they impact our Frame.

If our beliefs are based on **Not Good Enough** messages, they will become self-limiting beliefs. They will influence us to act in ways that are not in our Best Interest. They will hold us back and keep us stuck in places we would rather not be.

If our beliefs are based on **Good Enough** messages, they will become self-empowering beliefs. They will influence us to act in ways that are in our Best Interest. They will move us along a path that will help us develop our true potential.

**2. The Law of 'I Am':** A way to become aware of our own beliefs is to examine our self-talk and how we finish sentences that begin with the words 'I am.'

Student examples:  "I am going to fail this science test."
"I am able to figure out how to solve this problem."
"I am bored."

Teacher examples:  "I am going to have a miserable sixth period class."
"I am able to see this differently."
"I am not able to talk in front of the entire faculty."

Whatever we say after the words 'I am' seems to set our immediate future in motion. This is because of the **Law of I Am** which states that **whatever we say after we say I am is what we will become or experience.** It is as if a magical genie appears from the bottle ready and willing to grant our every wish.

Our lives can be compared to a tree and its root system. If the leaves of a tree are healthy, they are getting what they need from a strong root system. If the leaves are dying, the root system may not be providing what the tree needs to grow and produce fruit.

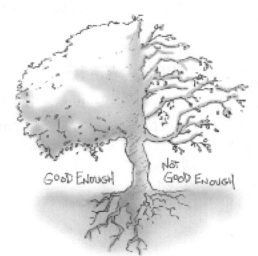

GOOD ENOUGH    NOT GOOD ENOUGH

Our lives have two parts to our root system. If we have received nurturing messages regarding our identity, worth and purpose, our *Good Enough* roots will grow and our tree will produce an abundance of fruit. This root system enhances our potential. Top 20s nourish these roots and have more productive lives and experiences.

However, if we have received negative messages regarding our identity, worth and purpose, our *Not Good Enough* roots will develop and our tree will not be productive. This root system limits our potential. Bottom 80s are often unaware of this root even though it has a negative influence on their lives and experiences.

Top 20 teachers understand this process in their own lives and in the lives of their students. Consequently, they send an abundance of messages to water the GE roots of their students, and they do what they can to whack away at the NGE roots.

Bethany Hamilton is a great example of the Law of I Am. Bethany is an outstanding athlete and marvelous surfer. At the age of 13, she was attacked by a shark and lost an arm. Within six months she was again surfing competitively and winning events.

Bethany did not have the *I Am* belief that she was an outstanding surfer because she had two arms. If she had held that belief, she would not have been able to continue surfing competitively after the shark attack. Rather, her 'I Am' belief is that "I am an outstanding surfer." This belief empowers Bethany to overcome obstacles that come her way, even the obstacle of losing an arm.

**3. The Law of Conviction:** The strength of our belief determines how real our belief feels to us. This in turn will determine the impact our belief will actually have on our life. Consequently, the **Law of Conviction** states that **the more we believe something to be true, the more real it feels for us.**

Pick a belief that you can relate to and personalize that belief.

> Examples:  I am highly unorganized.
> I am never going to understand this new computer program.

On the Conviction Scale, which number measures how much you believe it? This is your level of conviction. If your number is higher, you have a stronger conviction and that belief will have a greater influence on your life. If

WEAK    CONVICTION SCALE    STRONG
1  2  3  4  5  6  7  8  9  10

your number is lower, you have a weaker conviction and that belief will have a lesser influence on your life.

# REDUCING THE POWER OF NGE BELIEFS

We certainly would prefer to ward off NGE messages before they ever became a potential limiting belief. Being aware of the power of messages and their influence in forming beliefs might enable us to do just that. However, how can we deal with NGE beliefs that have already been formed? How can we reduce the power of NGE beliefs?

Top 20s diligently pay attention to their beliefs. They are especially attentive to beliefs when they are not getting the results they desire, when something in their life is not working the way they would like it to be working. It is in these situations that Top 20s are aware that an NGE or false belief is likely to be lurking.

Once they identify the belief, they reduce its power through a process called Name-Claim-Tame.

**1. Name It:** Top 20s not only identify the NGE belief, but they identify it **as a belief.** By naming it as a belief they know that it is not a fact. It is not something they can't do anything about, but it is something **in their thinking** that they can influence. Naming it as a belief is the first step in taking power to make a positive change.

**2. Claim It:** Top 20s understand the difference between who is responsible for a message and a belief. They realize that someone else may be responsible for the message, but they claim responsibility for the belief. Mary's professor is responsible for the message, "Mary, you should go back to high school and learn how to write." Mary, however, is responsible for accepting the message and holding on to the belief that she is a poor writer.

**Claiming the belief prevents us from blaming someone else for its existence.** Remember, by blaming someone else we would see ourselves as a victim, give up power to make a positive difference and stay stuck in the negative outcomes resulting from that belief. Claiming it as our own is the second step in taking power to make a positive change.

**3. Tame It:** Top 20s tame their NGE belief by taking direct action to weaken its conviction. Let's use the prior example, "I am never going to understand this new computer program," to see how this is done.

If a person identifies his conviction of this belief at a nine, it is unlikely that he would ever understand the new computer program. His NGE feelings would result in his avoiding working on the new program whenever possible. Once he **names it,** realizes that it is a belief and not a fact, and **claims it,** takes responsibility for the belief, he can then **tame it** by easing up on the conviction. **Easing up is an intentional effort by which he goes from a higher conviction to a lower conviction.** If he can do this, the weaker belief will no longer be an impediment to his learning the new program.

The following are examples of ease up tips that can be employed to weaken the negative power of a belief:

- **Say "Not now":** Whenever he is aware that he is having the belief, he can say "Not now" and send the belief away. If he doesn't say "Not now" and dwells on the belief, it will become stronger. By saying "Not now," he begins to take some control of the belief and gradually weakens its power.

- **Say "Maybe":** By saying "Maybe I will never understand this new computer program," he is not making a hard judgment but sending a message to himself that learning the new program is a possibility.

- **State the opposite:** Instead of saying, "I will never understand this new computer program," he can say, "I will figure out this new program." This may not *feel* comfortable or even seem possible, but it will prevent the NGE belief from being fueled.

- **Look for evidence that the belief may not be true:** He can realize that although there are parts of the computer program that he doesn't understand, there are some parts that he does understand. Maybe there is something that he understands now that he didn't understand yesterday.

- **Fake it 'til you make it:** He can pretend that he is able to learn the program and do what people who learn the program would do:
  - practice
  - read the training manual
  - ask for help

If he takes action and lowers his conviction from a nine to a five, gradually the NGE belief will have less negative influence in this situation. By continuing to ease up, he will lower his conviction even further. Before long he will be using the new program to assist him in his work. More important than being able to use the new computer program, however, is his confidence that he has internal power to make a positive difference in his life.

# THE BAMBOO TREE: PERSISTENCE

Whether aware of it or not, teachers are continually sending messages to their students. Consequently, teachers have a powerful influence in forming the beliefs young people have about their worth and potential. **Top 20 teachers realize that the most powerful things they bring into the classroom each day are the beliefs they have about their students and the messages they communicate to their students.**

Top 20 teachers recognize the NGE beliefs their students have of themselves and do what they can to change them. As important as this is, it is no easy task. The bamboo tree offers us an important lesson regarding this. If we plant a bamboo seed and water it and nurture it for a year, we will see no growth above the ground. Even if we did this for four years, we would see no growth. With these discouraging results, it would be easy to discontinue our efforts. But if we persisted and watered and nurtured where we had planted the seed, we could see 80 feet of growth in the fifth year. Although nothing was observed in the first four years, the bamboo's root system was growing underground. This enabled the rapid growth of the tree in the fifth year.

Top 20 teachers know that teaching requires the same persistence. Expressing a positive belief about a student once is wonderful, but empowering potential activating messages need to be sent again and again.

Do Top 20 teachers get frustrated when their students do not perform or learn or behave at the level at which they are capable? Of course they do. However, they overcome their frustration with a persistence to send GE messages that will take root in their students and become potential activating beliefs that empower young people to thrive in school and in life.

# TIME FOR REFLECTION & ACTION

1. Identify another person's opinion (OPO), expectation (OPE) or agenda (OPA) that has helped you remember the truth of who you are.

2. Identify a Not Good Enough message someone sent to you.

   A. Restate that message in the form of an 'I Am' belief: "I am _____."

   B. Based on the Conviction Scale, give it a number that corresponds to how strong the conviction of this belief is for you: _____

   C. Identify Ease Up actions (see p. 53 for examples) you could take to weaken the power of this belief.

3. What messages are you sending to your students or what beliefs do you have of your students that:

   A. Help them activate their potential?

   B. Block them from activating their potential?

4. What did you become aware of while reading this chapter regarding an action you would like to take? What action would you like to take?

# CHAPTER 6

# TOP 20 TEACHERS
# Create Connections

Spencer, an eighth grader, headed down the hallway to his last class of the day. He had successfully managed every class so far. He was good at the routine. Just walk into class, take a seat in the back, don't make eye contact or say anything, take a notebook out, don't do anything to disturb the teacher and everyone will leave you alone. After years of experience, Spencer knew just how to disengage and become invisible in school.

As he approached the classroom, he saw Miss Amatto standing at the door. "Hi, Spencer," she said as she handed him a yellow card. "I'm glad to see you're in my English class this semester."

"Hi, MiMatto," mumbled Spencer. As he took the yellow card and moved to the back of the room, he noticed that the desks were not in orderly rows. Instead, they were clumped together in groups of four.

The bell rang as Spencer plopped into the only empty seat. He recognized two of the boys sitting in his group. The third was a complete stranger.

The room quieted and Miss Amatto began talking. Spencer's mind wandered off to the video game he would spend hours on after school until he heard his teacher say, "Find the other three people who have the same color card as you and sit together in one of the groups of desks."

The students began moving around the room searching for their color-mates. Spencer's group, two girls and a boy, ended up sitting in the middle of the room. As the room quieted, Miss Amatto addressed the class. This time Spencer heard every word.

"This is an English class. English is a language. Although there are many different languages throughout the world, they all have the same purpose. They are all ways human beings can communicate so they can connect. This is a class about making connections. The two most important things we need in order to make connections are our name and our voice. So please bring those to class every day."

All the students laughed except Spencer who knew he would have to come up with a new strategy if he was going to remain invisible in Miss Amatto's class.

Miss Amatto is a Top 20 teacher. She not only expects her students to learn, but she prepares them for learning on the first day of class by beginning to build connections. She does this by greeting each student at the door and calling them by name. She forms them into small groups where their names and voices will matter and where they can gradually develop a feeling of belonging.

Students are categorized in many different ways when they come into school: third graders, sophomores, fifth hour class, bluebird reading group, student council, cheerleaders, soccer players, football captains, nerds, troublemakers and so on. But Top 20 teachers understand that **every student enters the school building each day as a person.** As such, there are things much more important to each of them than award stickers on their assignments, GPAs, pompoms and letter jackets.

The revolution in our classrooms will not require more books, computers or smart boards. Top 20 teachers know three more valuable resources that are crucial to student learning: name, voice and belonging.

**Name:** A student's name represents her identity. When someone speaks a student's name, she is identified. She is no longer a complete stranger in a strange land. The more often a student hears her name spoken in a respectful manner, the more likely she will be engaged in learning and other meaningful school activities. If a student does not hear her name in school or if it is spoken in a disrespectful manner, the more likely she will disengage. Unless a student hears her name spoken, she will not show up. Her body may be present but she will be disengaged. **Name matters.**

**Voice:** A student's voice represents his presence. When he speaks his voice, he is saying, "I am here." The longer a student's voice is not heard in a classroom, the more likely he will be disengaged from learning. His spoken voice indicates his arrival and willingness, at some level, to be engaged in what is going on in that room. **Voice matters.**

**Belonging:** Real learning requires openness. All learning is a going out from where we are to a new place. As such, learning is by its very nature risk-taking and a willingness to be vulnerable.

Belonging occurs when we are part of something larger than ourselves that is safe. This allows the student to take the risk to be open and vulnerable. Learning requires engagement and engagement requires energy. If a student does not perceive that she is in a safe environment, her energy will be directed towards self-preservation. Her energy will focus on protecting herself. She will withdraw and disengage from the learning process. Like a turtle in its shell, she will not risk being open and vulnerable or moving outside her Comfort Zone. She will not learn.

However, if she feels safe, her energy is not needed for self-preservation or protecting. She does not need to be defensive. Her energy can be directed towards self-enrichment. As such, she will engage in learning. **Belonging matters.**

## A PRIMARY ROLE OF THE TOP 20 TEACHER

Watch a newborn or toddler and you will witness the natural spirit of a child directed towards learning. Children this age do only two things: sleep and learn. If a child is not sleeping, he is learning. The spirit of a child is naturally geared towards learning. We do not have to teach this skill; children come wired this way. All we have to do is preserve this habit.

That spirit and desire for learning is so pronounced in two-year-olds that it tires out adults. We call that the *terrible twos*. That, however, is an adult description of a two-year-old. A two-year-old would describe this time in life as *it-doesn't-get-any-better-than-this*. That spirit would continue in a child if it didn't tire out adults. However, because we can't keep up with a *naturally spirited* child, we often dampen the spirit.

Sometimes there is good reason for this, like the child's physical safety. Nonetheless, adult responses to a child's natural spirit gradually take a toll on her curiosity. When the tender spirit of a child feels threatened, it begins to withdraw and the learning rate decreases.

**The Top 20 teacher's role is to re-connect the child to her natural spirit for learning.** In a sense, the teacher prepares the child for learning by *repairing* the child for learning. Essential to that preparation and reparation is the creation of physical and emotional safety. **It is only in that environment of safety where the natural spirit of the child will emerge again.** Like a plant that needs sunlight to flourish and grow, a child's curiosity is flourished by safety.

**Top 20 teachers deliberately prepare a student for learning by intentionally creating safety in the classroom.** This occurs when emotional connections are made. It occurs when name, voice and belonging matter.

# PODS: MAKING CONNECTIONS IN THE CLASSROOM

If a teacher asks a question in a typical classroom, the same three or four students seem to raise their hands all year. Generally only a fraction of the students participate in a classroom discussion.

**Pods is a classroom process that creates emotional connections through name, voice and belonging.** Pods is an intentional way of having each student's name and voice spoken every day and developing a sense of belonging among classmates.

**Set-up:**

1. Form Pods: If the classroom has desks, arrange the desks in groups of four. If the classroom has tables, arrange four chairs at each table.

2. Randomly assign four students to each Pod. This can be done in a number of ways.

   A. Colored cards: Have a stack of colored cards with four cards for each color. Have the number of cards match the number of students in the class. Randomly give each student a card. Those with the same color sit in the same Pod.

   B. Playing cards: Give each student a card from the deck. (If 24 students are in the class, only use cards 1-6; if 32 students are in the class, use cards 1-8.) Have students with the same number sit in the same Pod.

**Roles:** Each student is assigned a letter (A, B, C, D) and a corresponding task in the Pod for that day.

| | | |
|---|---|---|
| A = Asker | Repeats the teacher's question to other Pod members. | |
| B = First | Answers the question first. | |
| C = Scribe | Writes down each person's name and her answer to the question. | |
| D = Voice | Reports back to the large group using the Scribe's notes if necessary. | |

Note: Make a laminated sign of the four letters and the four roles. It's handy if the letters are attached to the sign by velcro so they can be easily moved. Post the sign on the wall in front of the room.

**Rules:**

1. Everyone gets to answer the question or pass.

2. Respect the speaker. Students are asked to turn their shoulders to the speaker. We cannot guarantee respect but we can ask our students to give the speaker their *shoulders*.

3. No *inter-podding*. Students from one Pod are not allowed to talk with students from another Pod during a discussion period. This is a way to insure that all Pod members feel that they matter to the group.

4. No Pod ripping. Students are informed that Pod groups are changed every six to seven class days (or whatever seems best for your class). This avoids offensive comments such as: "When are we ever going to change Pods?"

**Process:**

1. When the teacher asks a question for the Pods to answer, the Asker repeats the question to the group.

2. The student who is First answers the question first. Then, going clockwise, each student in the Pod answers the question.

3. The Scribe writes down each student's name and answer. He then hands that list to the Voice.

4. When called upon, the Voice shares the name and answer for each student. All students are asked to turn their shoulders to the Voice who is reporting.

The teacher changes the students' roles each time a Pod question is asked. D becomes the Asker; A is First; B is the Scribe; C is the Voice.

Note: Select one student (you may want to pick a student who is least likely to be engaged) to be the cheerleader. After each Voice reports the Pod responses to the question, the cheerleader says out loud, "1-2-3," and the other students clap once in unison.

Pods can be used once or several times during a class period. All Voices may not be called upon to report on every question or discussion. Nonetheless, every student's voice has been heard in the Pod.

## A TEACHER'S EXPERIENCE

Cori Pineda, an English teacher and student council advisor at Windsor High School in Windsor, Colorado, first heard of Pods at a Top 20 training session. After trying Pods, she sent the following email:

> "When I first heard about Pods, I thought, 'No, not for me. I'm a first year teacher. I can't get students to do this and be productive. I am supposed to keep them in their seats, silent and focused on me. That's what older, more experienced teachers say anyway.'
>
> "But my Leadership class was being disrespectful and chaotic. I tried Pods with them and IT WORKED! They were listening to one another, everyone was feeling heard, and we got done what we needed to do.
>
> "I'm now doing Pods with my freshman English class. We get so distracted with everyone's relating to what we're reading that we're falling behind. I looked into the heart of the matter and realized it's because **every student needs to be heard.** I need to honor that and realize that Pods are the way to do it."

Operating as a Top 20 teacher, Cori "looked into the heart of the matter." Her curiosity changed her Frame and resulted in her realizing that **every student needs to be heard.** By honoring that need, Cori created connections for her students and a more meaningful and productive learning experience for everyone.

## COMMUNICATING "YOU MATTER"

A fundamental way to create emotional connections is by communicating You Matter. We communicate You Matter to our students whenever we honor their needs. This happens in a special way when we honor their name, their voice and their need to belong.

Miss Amatto did this by having her students work in Pods, but she also communicated You Matter by greeting them at the door. Although a teacher's day is extremely busy and we may not be able to do it every day or every period, greeting our students at the door as they enter our classroom has a powerful impact. They are hearing their name, their voice is being heard and they are being treated as if they were someone special...and they are.

Tom now makes a habit of greeting students at the door. It has become an intentional, vital part of his curriculum. He might exchange a handshake, a high five or a smile along with the most beautiful sound in the world, the student's name.

One student, Richard, indicated the power of this ritual by stating that because Tom called him by name he was immediately drawn in to whatever learning experience was about to take place.

Jane, another student, says, "I am totally involved with any class where the teacher can make a one-to-one connection with me. I don't care if the subject is science, French or whatever, I will listen and do the work if I feel valued and connected."

Depending on the age of our students, we might greet them with a hug or some other meaningful gesture. We should also consider meeting them at the door when they leave our classroom on Fridays.

> **"People do not care how much you know until they know how much you care."**
> **–John Maxwell**

The honoring of name should extend past the boundaries of the classroom as well. The revolutionary Top 20 teacher greets the student the same way in the hallway, in the lunchroom, at the basketball game or at the mall. The message needs to be sent: "You matter to me as a person first, a learner second."

The ultimate sign of disrespect is not to notice someone. Although often unintentional, it communicates "You don't matter." No student should be unnoticed in our classrooms. No student should be invisible in our schools. No student should be left behind.

Top 20 teachers recognize that their students are persons and honor their names, their voices and their need to belong.

# TIME FOR REFLECTION & ACTION

1. How can you create connections in the classroom?

2. How do you communicate "You matter" to your students? How do you communicate "You don't matter"?

3. What did you become aware of while reading this chapter regarding an action you would like to take? What action would you like to take?

# CHAPTER 7

## TOP 20 TEACHERS
# Listen to Understand

It was one of those mornings for Mr. Morrissey, the guidance counselor at the high school. His daughter had been late getting ready for school, he had spilled coffee all over his pants and then he arrived in the school parking lot only to find no faculty spaces available. Once at his office, he found seven e-mails that needed his attention. Just then Leyla, a ninth grade student, knocked and asked if she could talk about her sophomore registration forms. "Sure, Leyla," said Mr. Morrissey, "my door is always open."

While Leyla explained her dilemma concerning science and math, her counselor continued answering the e-mails. Leyla paused before repeating the conflict in her schedule that needed to be ironed out before completing the forms.

"Yes, yes, we can do that," said Mr. Morrissey while shaking his head at the computer. The e-mail was from Mrs. Jackson, her third this week about her son.

"Now what did you say about Spanish class, Lisa?"

"Well, it's actually Leyla and Spanish isn't the problem."

Mr. Morrissey turned his Top 20 awareness on immediately, then shut his laptop and wheeled his chair toward her. "Totally my fault," he said, "I was not even close to listening to what you needed just then. If you wouldn't mind, could you please start over so I can help you?"

Leyla only **asked** for one thing from Mr. Morrissey but she really **needed** two. Not only did her schedule need attention, but she needed attention as well. She needed to know that she *mattered* while she communicated with her counselor.

Possibly no occupation on the planet requires more listening than that of teaching young people. Teachers' workdays are usually hectic, wall-to-wall stress-filled experiences. It is no easy task to give undivided attention to everyone who needs it. Still, it is our job to listen; it is our job to give attention. Teachers need to hear the voices of students, parents, administrators and peers…and they need to hear them clearly. If we want to know what's really going on in people we work with and teach, then we need to put ourselves into Top 20 listening mode.

**TRUE TALES**

Tom teaches a pre-algebra class. Recently, his students were struggling with ratios and percentages, topics students usually find quite simple. Quiz scores were low, student body language was negative and Tom could feel himself heading Below the Line. Instead of ranting and raving about the mathematics, he told the class to pack away their books and move the desks into a circle.

"Okay, here's the deal," stated Tom. "We are going to check in with each person and find out what's really going on. When we get to you, tell us how you are really doing…and we will listen to you."  One by one, the students took turns. Tom and the class listened intently. After just a minute or two, the answers became more and more real, intimate and revealing. Over half of the students shared extremely negative experiences involving family, peer or personal challenges. Three of the stories revealed serious situations that required referrals to the counselors.

The next day the atmosphere in the class was different. Homework was turned in and students were more engaged. Fifteen minutes of listening had conveyed the message that they *mattered*.

## LISTENING LEVELS

We sometimes get the improper notion that having two ears qualifies us as outstanding listeners. Although our listening is often dysfunctional, as in Mr. Morrissey's case, it may *feel* normal. Being aware of five levels of listening, Top 20 teachers can more effectively communicate with students and peers.

**1. My Life Is On My Mind.** Mr. Morrissey began his encounter with Leyla when he was operating from this Bottom 80 level. He had things in his life on his mind: his daughter, his

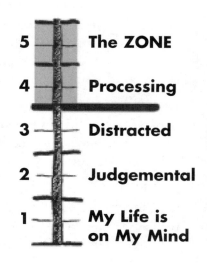

5 — The ZONE

4 — Processing

3 — Distracted

2 — Judgemental

1 — My Life is on My Mind

wet pants and his e-mails. Leyla's needs were physically present in his office, but her counselor was not really there.

> Have you had any of your life on your mind while you've been reading this book?

Thinking about our own life and its demands is normal and necessary. We just don't want to do that when it takes us away from being present in the moment and interferes with communicating effectively with others.

**2. Judgmental.** Sometimes we put on the robe, take out the gavel and turn into a judge. Had Mr. Morrissey's mind wandered into this level, he would have been thinking judgmental thoughts like:

- "Oh great, Leyla again. Here come five more headaches for me. Can't this kid just read the curriculum book?"

- "Science and math issues? What a surprise! Those are the worst two departments in our school."

- "If I can't solve her issue, I'm going to look like the lamest counselor in our office…again."

When we are judging, we are not listening. Judgment is a vital part of our lives, especially when we are making decisions while driving a car, caring for our own children or planning a lesson. Judging has a proper place in our day, but just not now when we need to be present in **this** moment. The formula is simple: listening should precede judging. As teachers we often judge before or during the listening.

> Have you made any judgments while reading this book?

**3. Distracted.** Falling victim to physical distractions can lead us to another form of Bottom 80 listening. Mr. Morrissey was distracted by his open laptop while Leyla was talking. We can all be distracted by noise in the hall, a warm spring day or a fly buzzing in the room.

> Have you had any physical distractions while reading this book?

**4. Processing.** This level can be a tricky one. When we are processing, we are listening like a tape recorder set on PLAY mode. As the other person is speaking, our poor listening is comprised of rapid-fire thinking creating solutions or responses for the issue at hand. Processing becomes a problem when we are answering the wrong questions. Sometimes our stenographer-like word-for-word listening robs us of the essence of the message that is being

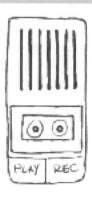

delivered to us in that moment. If Mr. Morrissey had been formulating solutions for Leyla while she was stating her problem, he'd most likely have missed the point of what she needed from him.

We need to turn the PLAY mode off on our internal tape recorder and push the RECORD button instead. Our listening should be so focused that we are not doing any problem solving or brainstorming during that part of the conversation. We should be simply listening. When the other person has finished speaking, there should be a short pause in the process. That pause is when our thinking should be switched into PLAY mode. Then and only then should we be offering ideas or suggestions to the other person.

**5. The Zone.** Top 20 teachers try to listen in the Zone as often as possible. In this level, they work hard to eliminate the other four levels and put themselves in the moment.

This is an addition by subtraction equation. When we eliminate Life on My Mind, Judgmental, Distracted or Processing modes, we automatically move to the Zone. It is as if the ballast bags are being cut off the hot air balloon. Once Mr. Morrissey shut down his laptop, turned his chair and zeroed in on Leyla's dilemma, he was listening in the Zone.

# GETTING TO THE ZONE

Awareness is indeed curative, but only if action is taken on the awareness. Research has shown that normal listeners drift off into Bottom 80 listening levels for one minute about 22 times per hour. This makes most of us (38 minutes out of 60 = 63%) below average listeners.

Distractions are part of life at school: bells ring, backpacks fall off desks, intercom announcements interrupt and notes arrive from the office. Top 20 teachers dive into Below the Line listening often, but they use their awareness to reduce the duration of those *day dreams*. They say to themselves, **"Not now,"** when they are distracted or catch themselves judging, processing or wandering off into thoughts about their own life. By saying *Not now,* they shorten their drifting time and focus on the present moment.

Sometimes *Not now* is an insufficient method in restoring focus and awareness. If we have major life issues on our mind, then Top 20 listening may be difficult or impossible to accomplish. In these cases, we can put our issues or challenges into our mental **Parking Lot**. Just as we leave our cars in the staff lot every morning and go back to them after school, we can place our distractions in a place where we can retrieve them later and deal with them more effectively. When our life challenges are so monumental that we cannot *park* them for a while, then it is probably time for us to take a mental health day and get a substitute teacher.

# THE ZONE AND OTHER AREAS OF OUR LIFE

Knowing the five listening levels can be helpful in other areas as well. There are times when our Bottom 80 focus levels prevent us from accomplishing what is in our Best Interest:

- **Reading:** We can read four pages in a novel only to realize that, because we were distracted or had life on our mind, we have no recollection of what was read. A simple *Not now* might get us back on track the next time our mind wanders while reading.

- **Performing:** It is difficult to perform the professional tasks of a teacher when we are not in the Zone. Delivering a lesson, conducting a practice or speaking to parents on the telephone can be ineffective experiences when our thinking is not focused.

- **Sleeping:** We fall asleep only when we are in the Zone! Distractions, judgments and life on our mind keep our mind racing and keep us awake.

- **Relationships:** Becoming aware and acting on these listening levels can have a profound impact on our relationships, both professional and personal. Listening in the Zone may be hard work but it immediately communicates You Matter to the speaker.

Often in our roles as teachers or mentors, it is our task to help our students gain important insights about their lives. Sometimes we may offer helpful suggestions or advice, but there are times when those pearls of wisdom are not sufficient. The most meaningful *insights* come from the *inside* not the *outside*. The best way for a student or peer to gain such an insight is to talk with someone who really listens to him. This can be the most powerful form of counseling that teachers give: an empathetic ear.

# TIME FOR REFLECTION & ACTION

1. Identify a time when your poor listening had a negative impact for you as a teacher.

2. Identify an area in your life where you want to be more aware of your listening levels. Before entering this area next time, remind yourself to *just listen.*

3. What did you become aware of while reading this chapter regarding an action you would like to take? What action would you like to take?

# CHAPTER 8

## TOP 20 TEACHERS

# Help Students Move Outside Their Comfort Zone

Mr. Moss taught middle school science and coached a girls' basketball team. One day he asked Kendra, a sixth grader on his team, to stay after practice. "Kendra, I know you want to play basketball in high school. I think you would be more successful at that level if you could dribble left-handed. Let's practice that a bit."

"I've tried that, Coach, but I always lose the ball."

"Sure, but with a little practice, that won't happen." He spread a number of chairs at different places on the court and tossed her a ball. "Try dribbling with your left hand around those chairs."

Before she got to the second chair, she lost control of the ball. When she heard two boys in the gym laughing, she said, "This won't work, Coach. I can't do this."

"Kendra, every day in practice I want you to have a basketball in your hands. Whenever we're not doing something else, I want you dribbling the ball with your left hand. If you're standing in line or even sitting on the bench, just dribble the ball with your left hand."

After practice a week later, Mr. Moss set up the chairs again. When he tossed Kendra the ball, she knew what he wanted her to do. Slowly she weaved her way around the chairs until she got to the other end of the court.

"What do you think?" he yelled.

Dribbling back towards him, she said with a smile on her face, "I need more practice."

He sat on the bench as she dribbled around the chairs. A few times she fumbled the ball, but hustled to pick it up and kept going. After ten minutes he said, "That's enough for today. We will pick it up again tomorrow."

Kendra walked off the court towards the locker room...dribbling the ball with her left hand.

Everyone needs a Comfort Zone, that place where we're safe and secure and we know how to do what we have to do. However, developing our potential or the potential of our students requires moving outside the Comfort Zone. That's where we find the Big Learning.

> "A ship in port is safe, but that's not what ships are built for."
> **Grace Murray Hopper**

# STUCK INSIDE COMFORT ZONE

Small children seem to naturally move outside their Comfort Zone. That's why so much learning goes on in the early years. But as they get older, they become more reluctant to wander into uncharted territory. Why do some people, adults as well as children, become stuck inside their Comfort Zone?

**1. Fear of OPOs:** OPOs are Other Peoples' Opinions. Because we often think our value and worth come from other people, we do those things that will gain the approval of others and avoid those things that will garner their disapproval. We operate as if we have radar screens on top of our heads that zero in on what others approve of and what they don't.

How much power did Kendra give the two boys who laughed at her when she fumbled the basketball? Was it because of them that she told Mr. Moss that she couldn't learn how to dribble left-handed? Was it their opinion of her that would have kept her locked inside her Comfort Zone?

Other Peoples' Opinions are powerful, especially in our students' lives. Opinions of others can also be valuable to our students. Top 20 teachers help their students make decisions about OPOs based on Best Interest.

If OPOs are in a student's Best Interest, he should listen to them.

> Example: "I think you would be more successful playing basketball in high school if you could dribble left- handed."

If OPOs are not in a student's Best Interest, he shouldn't listen to them.

> Example: "Doing homework is a waste of time."

**2. Fear of Failure:** Possibly the most damaging belief that has crept into the mind of 21st century America is that failure is a bad thing that has to be avoided at all costs. This fear and belief has imprisoned countless adults in their Comfort Zone. Unfortunately, this fear and belief make their way into students' minds at way too early an age.

> "The greatest mistake you can make in life is to be continually fearing you will make one."
> –Elbert Hubbard

**Failure is an event, not a person.**

Failure is something we do; it is not who we are. Failure is a necessary part of every person's natural development. Trying develops potential. If a baby never tried to crawl, she would never crawl. When she first tries to crawl, she fails. She tries again and fails. This behavior is repeated countless times. It is by trying that the baby's **potential** to crawl is developed into her **ability** to crawl.

The same is true for Kendra. If she never tried to dribble left-handed, she would never develop the ability to dribble left-handed. But by trying and failing, her potential to dribble left-handed developed into her ability to dribble left-handed.

Failure is the great mother of learning. Can you think of any human invention that did not result from human failure? Thomas Edison failed hundreds of times before he figured out the light bulb. Prior to his success, Edison had been urged to do something else with his career. His response to his earlier failures, however, was that each failure brought him one step closer to figuring out how he could achieve his goal.

> "Mistakes are the portals of discovery."
> –James Joyce

**Success happens when people learn enough from failure and try one more time.**

## RESPONSES FROM OTHERS TO OUR FAILURES AND MISTAKES

It is believed that infants have only two natural fears: the fear of falling and the fear of loud noises. All other fears are learned. The fear of failure and the fear of making mistakes are learned from the responses other people make to us when we fail or make a mistake.

We have asked thousands of students and adults how others (parents, teachers, coaches, siblings, peers) responded to them when they were youngsters and they made a mistake. Their responses are extremely consistent among all age groups:

- Laughed
- Ridiculed
- Teased
- Were disappointed
- Were angry

- Yelled
- Gave the 'look'
- Kept bringing it up
- Punished
- Told others

- Shamed
- Judged
- Criticized
- Freaked out
- Lost trust

Occasionally, though rarely, people say that others responded by helping, supporting or encouraging them when they failed or made a mistake.

But if these negative responses are the norm, the message is loud and clear: "YOU BETTER NOT MAKE A MISTAKE." It is because of the frequency and likelihood of these responses that people fear failure and mistake-making. As a result, they fear moving outside their Comfort Zone and handicap their learning and potential.

## THE POPCORN STORY

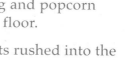

When Paul was seven years old, he wanted to make popcorn. While his parents were in the living room, he undertook his cooking adventure in the kitchen. He put oil into a pot and placed it on the hot burner. Once the oil was hot, Paul reached up to pour popcorn seeds into the pot. Unfortunately, when the plastic bag containing the seeds touched the hot pot, a hole melted in the bag and popcorn seeds spilled all over the stove, counter and floor.

Upon hearing this commotion, Paul's parents rushed into the kitchen and immediately asked, "Are you OK?"

"Yes," Paul answered. Although startled by what had happened, he had not been burned.

"Are you sure?"

"Yes, I'm fine," Paul replied.

"Good," said his parents, "we'll help you clean up the mess."

Paul's popcorn mistake and the way his parents responded made a powerful mental and emotional imprint on him and resulted in his learning four important lessons.

**1. People are more important than a mistake.** Because his parents' immediate concern was for his well-being and not for the popcorn mess, Paul experienced deep value and worth.

**2. Be there when people mess up.** One of our purposes in life is to help others when they experience difficulties. It is our responsibility not to clean it up for them, but to support them in making things better.

**3. There is a lesson in the mistake.** In Paul's case the lesson is that heat melts plastic. Every mistake or failure offers an important life lesson.

**4. Mistakes and failure are wonderful.** Because many wonderful things can be learned from mistakes and failure, they are to be valued, not avoided. It is the **belief** that they are beneficial that makes them beneficial for Top 20s. It is the **belief** that they are to be avoided that results in them not being beneficial for Bottom 80s.

Paul's parents responded to him when he made the popcorn mistake by affirming him and his worth. As wonderful as that response is, unfortunately it isn't common.

# THE FLASHLIGHT STORY

Michael Cole had a very different experience regarding mistake-making.

Although not an electrician, seven-year old Michael's father tried to repair wiring in his own home. Since the electricity to the house had to be turned off while his father worked on the wiring, young Michael's job was to hold the flashlight so his father could see. If his father couldn't get something to work, he would always rage and swear at Michael for how he was holding the flashlight, "Michael, you're good for nothing. You never do anything right." If his father became displeased a second time, the punishment would become even more severe.

The messages sent to young Michael were certainly different than those sent to Paul.

**1. You're not good enough.** He was told that he was inadequate and couldn't do anything right.

**2. Please others or else.** Trouble and pain result from not pleasing other people and nothing short of perfection is acceptable.

**3. Confusion about mistakes and failure.** Michael didn't even make a mistake but, because of the message he got in this experience, went through life sometimes believing things were mistakes when they weren't.

**4. The lesson is in the punishment.** Whereas Paul learned that a lesson was in the mistake, Michael learned that the lesson was in the punishment. Every mistake needed to have some sort of a punishment attached to it.

It wasn't until the age of 48 when Michael heard Paul's popcorn story that his Frame changed, and he realized there was another way of seeing mistakes. He discovered he could learn valuable lessons from mistakes without needing punishment.

> "If I had my life to live over...I'd dare to make more mistakes next time."
> –Nadine Stair

## OUR RESPONSES TO MISTAKES

Whether we are aware of it or not, we respond in some way to every mistake we make. How we respond to our own mistakes is largely influenced by how others have responded to us when we have failed. These responses fall into four Bottom 80 ways and one Top 20 way.

1. We **deny** a mistake by verbally or mentally stating, "It didn't happen." We don't talk about it. We block it out of our mind. If someone else brings it up, we deny it or get defensive.

2. We acknowledge the mistake but **blame** someone else for it. This may take the form of "He did it" or "She made me do it." We blame in order to get off the hook, but in blaming we avoid responsibility.

3. We **justify** the mistake. We make excuses or offer good reasons for making the mistake. "I didn't get my assignment done because I had to go to my grandmother's birthday party." If we can be convincing, we won't be the recipients of any of the negative responses that were covered earlier.

4. We **dwell** on it by focusing on nothing else but the mistake. We allow the mistake to overwhelm us and define us: "I'm so stupid. I never do anything right. I'll never be able to get over this."

5. We **own** it by looking the mistake squarely in the eye. We take responsibility and learn the lesson life is trying to teach us. We use the mistake as a teacher: "I just made a mistake. What can I learn from this?"

> "I have learned throughout my life as a composer chiefly through my mistakes...not by my exposure to fonts of wisdom and knowledge."
> –Igor Stravinsky

When we operate like a Bottom 80 and respond to mistakes and failures by denying, blaming, justifying or dwelling, we are likely to repeat the mistake over and over again. Life will offer us many opportunities to learn.

Teachers will observe these four Bottom 80 responses if they look closely enough in their classrooms. After a poor performance on a math exam, it is common to hear students say:

- **Denying:** "I didn't get this part wrong. This isn't a decimal point here. It's a period."

- **Blaming:** "I failed because you taught this wrong. My friend's teacher did this lesson better."

- **Justifying:** "I got an F, but I have been doing service projects for my social justice class."

- **Dwelling:** "I don't believe how stupid I am. This is a disaster. I will never get into college now."

By responding as a Top 20 who owns and learns from failures, we are not likely to repeat them. Since the purpose of mistakes is to learn a lesson, once the lesson is learned, the need to focus on the mistake no longer exists.

We will see this behavior occasionally in our students, but only those who are aware that owning mistakes and learning from them is a Top 20 habit:

- **Owning:** "Wow, I really blew this part of the test. I'm going to get help from my friend. Then I'll see my teacher before school tomorrow to figure this out."

# A.C.T.

What can teachers do to help students minimize their fear of failure or mistakes and encourage them to move outside their Comfort Zone? How do Top 20 teachers A.C.T.?

**A**ware: Top 20 teachers are aware of their own beliefs about themselves as mistake makers and their own beliefs about failure. The purpose of this awareness is not to condemn people from their past who may have influenced this belief. Rather, it is to be aware of their own beliefs so they know what will get activated within them when they or someone else makes a mistake.

**C**onscious Choices: Top 20 teachers make two conscious choices. **The first conscious choice regards how they want to respond when they make a mistake.** They realize that if they don't make a conscious choice, they are likely to make an unconscious choice. Those unconscious choices are likely to involve denying, blaming, justifying or dwelling.

**The conscious choice that Top 20 teachers make is to own the mistake and learn the lesson.** If this doesn't come naturally for us, we can create our own script. A script is the specific words we say when a certain cue occurs. The cue in this situation is that a mistake has been made. A Top 20 script would sound something like this:

"Oops, look what I just did. I wonder what I can learn from this."

- "Oops" indicates that a mistake has been made.
- "Look what I just did" reveals a willingness to own the mistake and take responsibility for it.
- "Wonder what I can learn from this" reveals the Top 20 teacher's curiosity to learn the lesson.

**The second conscious choice Top 20 teachers make is how to respond to others, especially children, when they make a mistake.** Again, without making a conscious choice, we are likely to make an unconscious choice and respond with one of those negative responses on page 72.

Having a script for this conscious choice can also be helpful. A Top 20 script might sound something like, "Hmmm, what can we learn from this?"

**T**alk: Top 20 teachers talk about their own mistakes and failures. Paul once served on the administrative team of a high school. The school administrator sometimes said at a meeting, "I made a decision that was a mistake. I want to talk about this and have you help me learn everything I can from this mistake so I will do it better next time."

That's the attitude of a Top 20 leader most of us would be very willing to follow. Furthermore, it creates an atmosphere for others to talk about and learn from their mistakes.

Top 20 teachers willingly and openly acknowledge their own mistakes in their classrooms. This vulnerability opens the door to students to do the same and safely leave their Comfort Zones.

## NO NEUTRAL RESPONSE TO A MISTAKE

Participants at a Top 20 training session listed several negative responses to mistakes like those on page 72. The group was then asked, "What happens to a child when she receives these responses?" A fourteen-year-old girl responded, "It's the end of innocence."

The wisdom from this young person reveals that **there is no neutral response to a mistake.** Children go through life wide open. When they make a mistake, they naturally learn from it. If parents or teachers respond to that mistake in a positive way, children will continue to be open. But if the response is negative, they begin to close up. In either case, whether it is a 'popcorn' type response, a 'flashlight' type response, or a mixture of the two, it makes a difference in children's lives. Because Top 20 teachers understand this, they respond to their students' mistakes and failures in ways that encourage them to go outside their Comfort Zone.

> "Freedom is not worth having if it does not include the freedom to make mistakes."
> –Mahatma Gandhi

## TIME FOR REFLECTION & ACTION

1. What messages did you receive as a youngster when you made a mistake? What belief about yourself as a mistake-maker did these messages form in you?

2. How do OPOs (Other Peoples Opinions) and the Fear of Failure affect you regarding staying inside your Comfort Zone?

3. Make a conscious choice and create a script for yourself when:

   A. You make a mistake.

   B. A child or student makes a mistake.

4. What did you become aware of while reading this chapter regarding an action you would like to take? What action would you like to take?

# CHAPTER 9

## TOP 20 TEACHERS
# Answer the Relevancy Question: "What's in It for Me?"

TRUE TALES

Kelsey approached Tom's desk during her Algebra 2 class and slammed the book down on his desk. "I don't understand any of this," she said. "I'm frustrated, overwhelmed and I don't see the point of doing this synthetic division. I'm not sure what my future will be, but it won't involve any of this stuff."

Tom was tempted to go back to his old script in answering Kelsey's frustrated comments. In his early years of teaching, he would have said, "It's too bad this is difficult. You need the content for the ACT test and the grades to get into college…and you need to do it because I'm telling you to do it."

Pausing for a split second, he took a deep breath and responded, "I know you are interested in the fine arts and drama. Right, Kelsey?" She nodded quizzically. "Is there ever a time in a play where you are really confused about how to act a certain role?" Again, she nodded. "Then that's what synthetic division is all about for you in this class," he continued. "You're right. You will most probably never use this specific content anywhere in your future if you concentrate on the fine arts. But what you will use is persistence, self-discipline and the willingness to ask for help when you need it. You are developing all three of these Star Qualities every day in math class."

"But I am getting a C+ in here," she complained. "I could probably get an A or B if I switched to an easier course next trimester."

Now Tom nodded. "What will help you more in your future career, a good grade in an easy class or picking up Star Qualities in a tougher class?"

Like Kelsey, more and more students are asking the question: "What's in it for me? When am I ever going to need this?" Young learners have unlimited access to learning materials outside the classroom (television, computers, cell phones). Many tech-savvy students claim that they are getting more beneficial learning after school than during school. Because Top 20 teachers are armed with a new understanding of relevancy, they offer a meaningful response to the "What's in it for me?" question.

# MOUNTAIN OF LEARNING: CONFUSION ROCKS!

Traditionally, teachers present content information to students who are expected to learn it. Although educators are taught many approaches and styles of teaching, we seldom share with our students the process of learning.

Learning can be compared to climbing a mountain. The bottom of the mountain represents the stage where a student does not yet know or understand the content being taught. Here a student would say, "I don't get it." The top of the mountain represents the *Aha* stage when a student has learned or understood the content. Here a student would say, "Aha! I get it now."

Although students understand this, many are unaware of the middle part of the journey. As they climb the mountain towards the *Aha*, they encounter confusion. Top 20 students realize that they must work through confusion in order to get the learning. They see confusion as a natural part of learning. Unfortunately, when Bottom 80 students experience confusion, they stop climbing: "I don't get it. I'm confused. I must be stupid. I quit." Students who believe that being confused means that they are not good enough quit the learning process.

**All learning requires passing through confusion.** Small children experience confusion when they are trying to walk or learning to speak. However, since they don't equate confusion as being negative, they continue on the learning path.

Confusion needs to be part of our curriculum. We need to teach our students about confusion so they understand it as the stage that happens right before *Aha*. Realizing this, students will not acticvate their Not Good Enough belief when they are confused. (Confusion will be revisited in Chapter 10.)

## MEMORIZATION OR REALIZATION

Many students turn off to some of their classes because of confusion, but other factors also cause their disengagement. Memorization was a skill that suited students very well in school a generation ago. The ability to take in information, store it and later repeat that information back to the teacher generally resulted in good grades from elementary school through college.

Tom was one of those students who greatly benefited from this rote system of learning. Having a good memory, he could *rent* information readily and find a temporary *warehouse* to store it in his head until he delivered it back to the teacher. Since there was no apparent further use for this information after Tom attained his award stickers and A+ grades, he could dump or erase the data from his memory bank.

While Tom was able to easily memorize the Gettysburg address ("Four score and seven years ago, our forefathers...."), he had no grasp whatsoever of the significance of that Civil War event. This doesn't discount the importance of knowing the text in the Gettysburg address. However, it would be better to know its meaning. Because students today can access the complete text of Lincoln's famous speech in a matter of seconds, delivering data to be memorized is no longer a teacher's primary purpose.

**Top 20 teaching is more about Realizations than Memorization.** We want to develop learners who *own* (not rent) the concepts we teach and retain (not erase) them far beyond the evaluation phase. Often memorization involves 'small' learning (how to spell 'integrity') while realization involves 'big' learning (how to live with integrity).

> A student in Mrs. Kapur's class had to memorize the state capitals for geography. Knowing that a realization would make a much longer-lasting impression than a memorization, the teacher did a role-play for the students. "Does anyone know the capital of Colorado?" she asked. Several students quickly answered, "Denver."
>
> "But does anyone know why Denver became the state's capital? Think of the pioneers traveling west towards California in the 1800's. They had taken wagons from the east all the way across the Great Plains. They were exhausted and so were their oxen pulling the wagons. Once they made it halfway across Colorado, they ran right into the Rocky Mountains. You can imagine why so many settlers abandoned their California hopes and settled at the foot of these seemingly impassable slopes. Denver is the capital because so many pioneers ended their journeys there."

Although there will always be a place for some memorization in the learning process for our students, realizations ought to be our goal. Realizations, which offer students connections in their learning, will allow students to apply their learning to situations that are meaningful in their lives.

## LEARNING 'IN THE MOMENT' AND 'AFTER THE FACT'

How do we get students to these *Aha* moments? Two different paths lead up the mountain. Some learners get these light bulbs turned on **In the Moment** (ITM). After just one example of a math problem, some students understand the concept being presented. The light bulb doesn't come on for other students in that same class until they see multiple examples or do their homework later that night. These are **After the Fact** (ATF) learners. An ITM learner in first period math class could very well be an ATF learner in second period English class. If realizations are important, then neither ITM nor ATF is a better method of learning. They are simply d-i-f-f-e-r-e-n-t.

Elementary school students, especially in their earlier grades, mostly learn ITM. Teachers rarely expect youngsters to leave the classroom puzzled and then go home and unravel the mysteries of learning on their own. There's nothing wrong with this ITM method. It is a developmentally appropriate way to teach third graders.

Ten years later in college, students learn in vastly different ways. Most learning at the university level occurs outside of the lecture hall. Students are routinely expected to master concepts on their own or in study groups at the library or coffee shop. These ATF realizations are a major part of the learning process that carries into the real world where very few ITM realizations occur in parenting children or dealing with work issues.

| ITM<br>LEARNING | ATF<br>LEARNING |
|:---:|:---:|
| GRADE SCHOOL<br>**75%** | GRADE SCHOOL<br>**25%** |
| HIGH SCHOOL<br>**50%** | HIGH SCHOOL<br>**50%** |
| COLLEGE<br>**25%** | COLLEGE<br>**75%** |

If third grade is primarily ITM learning and college is mostly ATF learning, then what should be happening in our middle schools and high schools? Half of the learning in grades seven through twelve should come In the Moment and the other half After the Fact. **Top 20 teachers are aware of this and they tell their students about it!**

But here's the problem. Students who are not aware that the 'rules' for learning are changing, immediately go to Bottom 80 responses to this confusing time in their education. When they no longer get immediate ITM learning, they routinely:

- Blame others, especially their teachers.
- Turn the "I'm bored" switch on.
- Procrastinate doing the necessary work.
- Turn their brains off and quit.

Although this situation has always existed in middle and high schools, with the explosion of the tech age it has become even more pronounced. Dr. David Walsh, a leading expert on teenage brain development and technology, notes that 21st century students expect their entertainment and the rest of their lives to be "more, fast, easy and fun." Expecting the same at school, they are sadly disappointed when teachers don't deliver the same *punch* as their favorite video game.

Once teachers make students aware that confusion is a natural part of the learning process, they are far more likely to stay engaged in the classroom. **The Top 20 teacher brings out the Top 20 student.** On the way up the mountain, through confusion and en route to the ATF Aha at the top, students then routinely:

- Own and take responsibility for learning.
- Look for relevancy and realizations when they don't see either.
- Keep their brains on.
- Know that they just haven't learned it *yet*.

When Top 20 students haven't learned ITM, they know where to get the *not yet bus* for ATF realizations. They get to their teachers for extra help, join a study group after school or try doing their homework. Going to the mall or a football game is a wonderful activity for a high school student, but they're the wrong bus stops for an ATF Aha.

If our goal is truly to educate young people, then we must find ways to reward After The Fact learning by our students. A wise administrator once asked Tom, "Are you trying to get them to graph parabolas by December 3rd at 1:30 p.m., or are you trying to get them to graph parabolas?" If learning is still valuable ATQ (After The Quiz) or ATT (After The Test), then we need to figure out how to evaluate and honor that experience. Re-testing and extra credit projects are options Top 20 teachers consider.

## BUT WHAT'S IN IT FOR ME?

Realizations alone, or learning for the sake of learning, are not enough to attract the interest of many young students. Bottom 80 attitudes are alive and well in our schools. Students routinely say to their teachers:

- "Why are we doing this?"
- "This is stupid."
- "We've learned this before."
- "When am I ever going to use this?"

Students who fail to see (or even look for) relevancy in their courses are prone to boredom, procrastination and various other forms of rebellion. They quit. Some actually leave school but many don't go away. Day after day, they sit in their desks daydreaming and disengaged. This was not always the case in their education. Many of these checked-out students were once curious learners in their early grade school days.

When students are in their Top 20 mode, they are always on the lookout for relevancy. Although they may feel held captive in school for seven hours a day and 180 days a year, Top 20s know that they can keep their power in this situation by finding *what's in it for me*. They stay curious and look for the Big Three relevant factors in their education: Content and Grades, Intellectual Muscle Building and Star Qualities.

## CONTENT AND GRADES

Specific course content is an incentive for a handful of students in every classroom. Of 30 students in a science class five or six might be really interested in the course content. A budding pharmacist, veterinarian, astronomer or nurse may be sitting in the second row of a chemistry class, but in the next row sit future poets, counselors, waitresses and stay-at-home fathers. Some will benefit directly from balancing oxygen equations, but most will not.

Listen to Tom's personal realization about students and content:

"I used to give what I thought was an extremely motivational speech every fall. I'd hold up a set of keys and tell my students that math was the key to their future. Algebra would allow students to acquire keys that would open doors for them down the road. These keys could actually lead to a career as an insurance actuary! Very few students seemed to care much for this talk, but, undeterred, I cranked out this message for 25 years. It's now apparent to me that very few students connect the content they are learning today with what they will do in the future. Their future seems to extend as far as lunchtime or the hockey game that evening, but definitely not to becoming an actuary. I have put the key speech away for good."

Course content is important. Pharmacists need a solid background in chemistry and social workers need to understand group dynamics. The problem comes when teachers sell their content as the only available learning product in their classrooms. Today's students can attain some of this content through alternative, tech-driven methods, many of which are more effective and 'edu-taining' than traditional classroom lessons. These students are demanding more than content as they learn.

Grades have always served as a huge incentive for students. "Turn this paper in by Friday or you'll be lowered one grade," warns the teacher, hoping to motivate his students. "If you don't listen during this lecture, you won't get an A on the exam."

Grades are effective motivators for the small percentage of students who excel and earn the high grades. How many teachers would enjoy a system where the administrators would publish the grades and rankings for all the teachers on their staff each week? The top five teachers might applaud this system, just as the five fastest runners in the school would enjoy a daily hundred-yard dash competition. But what about the rest of the people who get the C+ grades and finish well back in the pack in every race? Grades are certainly not motivation for every learner.

Sparky, a seal at Como Zoo in St. Paul, Minnesota, does a show every summer day. A talented sea lion, Sparky honks horns, fetches rubber rings and claps his flippers on command. Every time he performs one of these feats, he is rewarded with a fish from the trainer's bucket. Many times, our school system looks all too similar to this zoo. We train students to do educational tricks (papers, projects, homework problems) by motivating them with grades. But grades, like class content, are not the chief motivators for a large majority of today's young learners. We have to offer these students something more.

## BUILDING INTELLECTUAL MUSCLE

Most high school weight rooms are jam-packed with students after school. Once there, they engage in bench-pressing weights, riding stationary bikes and running on treadmills. These seemingly meaningless activities bear strong relevance to students and athletes. They can easily relate lifting a small iron bar to building biceps and forearm muscles. One activity has relevance to another. Wrestlers know that weightlifting provides them with physical strength in a future match. Some young people hit the weight room to develop muscles for athletics, others just to maintain a healthy lifestyle.

We need to teach students that the same is true in our classrooms. We are building strength in math, English and Spanish class each day, just like the weight room. However, this strength has nothing to do with biceps. The most important muscle development in youngsters occurs in the six-inch space between their ears: Intellectual Muscle. No matter what the future holds for these students, they will use their thinking muscle more than their forearm muscles. Life is about problem solving. Careers are about problem solving. Those with poorly developed intellectual muscle will have a difficult time surviving and thriving.

Top 20 teachers reveal to students that brain-building exercises are available in their classrooms every day.

> "Okay, I see how doing these twenty sentences in grammar class would be good practice," says Jake, a newly informed Top 20 student. "I might even get an ATF realization out of this assignment. But if I've already mastered these skills, why should I bother doing all this?"
>
> Ms. Loch, a Top 20 teacher, knew just what to tell Jake. "Don't you already know how to make a layup in basketball? I saw you take twenty before last night's game. I'll bet Tiger Woods is practicing hundreds of seven-iron swings on the golf range today. It's all about building muscle with repetition, Jake."

Students need to realize that regular workouts of their Intellectual Muscle and other body muscles prepare them to succeed in the classroom and on the field.

## STAR QUALITIES: THE HIDDEN CURRICULUM

Content, grades and problem solving skills may not apply to every student, but Star Qualities do. These are the personal development character traits that young people acquire as they mature into young adults. Star Qualities like responsibility, self-motivation, organization and patience are certainly desired outcomes for our young learners. They're the primary reason Top 20 teachers enter the classroom each day.

Embedded within our classroom activities and content and buried beneath the social studies maps or the science periodic table, lies a *hidden curriculum*. Specific content outcomes are measurable and important components of our curriculum but so are Star Qualities. Science class might be where a student develops persistence as she needs to repeat a lab assignment. World cultures class might be where a student develops perspective as he sees things from other points of view. English class might be where a student develops the ability to ask for help because she can't grasp Shakespeare on her own.

Tom's son, Shane, was in the trumpet section of his school jazz band that practiced every Tuesday morning before school from 6:30 – 7:30. While Shane will not be performing at Carnegie Hall in the near future, he did develop the Star Quality of getting-out-of-bed-when-I-don't-feel-like-it. This skill has served him well as a math teacher with a forty-minute commute. Five days a week Shane's alarm goes off at 5:30 a.m., and he uses the Star Quality he developed in high school to get to work on time.

Neither Shane nor our students can stop by a drive-thru restaurant and ask for an order of self-confidence or motivation. Star Qualities can't be found there, but they can be found in students' classes and co-curricular activities. Top 20 teachers let their students in on the big secret: Star Qualities are here for the taking. *Don't leave school without them.*

Students might ask, "When am I ever going to use Spanish verb endings?" However, they will never ask, "When am I ever going to use self-confidence, motivation or organization?"

In addition to developing Star Qualities, Top 20 teachers also help students reduce Negative Mental Habits that become roadblocks to success in school and life. By increasing a student's self-confidence, a Top 20 teacher reduces self-doubt. By reducing a student's apathy, a teacher increases motivation. By combating negative habits like boredom, procrastination, sarcasm, pessimism, worry, guilt and anger, Top 20 teachers make a huge difference in students' lives. This may not have been part of the curriculum years ago, but it's part of the Top 20 teacher's lesson plan every day.

# TIME FOR REFLECTION & ACTION

1. Regarding what you are teaching, how can you help students make realizations?

2. How can you reward students who are learning ATF (after the test or after the assignment is due)?

3. What impact do grades have on your students?

4. Identify the IQ name and the EQ name for your class. The IQ name is the traditional name for your class (math, health, reading). The EQ name would be the Star Qualities your students would develop by being in your class.

Examples: IQ name is Health     EQ name is Decision Making

IQ name is Art     EQ name is Perspective

Note: If your students are not interested in the content of your class, suggest to them that they cross out the IQ name for the class on their notebooks and replace it with an EQ name.

5. Check the list of Star Qualities in Appendix A.

6. What did you become aware of while reading this chapter regarding an action you would like to take? What action would you like to take?

## TOP 20 TEACHERS
# Keep Stupid in the Box

Mrs. Hernandez had just returned yesterday's test to her fifth grade math class when Bobby raised his hand.

"Mrs. H, you wrote NY at the top of my paper. Does that mean New York?"

"NY means *Not Yet*. It means you haven't learned how to add fractions yet."

"Does that mean I failed the test?" Bobby asked. "I must be stupid."

"Remember when you were younger and didn't know how to ride a bike? You used training wheels. Did it ever cross your mind then that you were stupid or were failing?"

"No, I don't think so, Mrs. H."

"When you didn't know how to ride a bike yet, what did you do?"

"I guess I kept trying until I finally got it."

"That's right. There was no thought of stupid or failing. You just kept trying until you got it. That's why we're going to practice adding more fractions today."

One of the greatest roadblocks to a student's success is his belief that he **is** stupid. This belief stems from the student's repeated **feelings** of being stupid. As these feelings of stupid get stacked, they form a belief of stupid. When this occurs, a student's chance for success is greatly diminished.

Had Mrs. Hernandez put an 'F' on Bobby's test paper, he may have experienced feeling stupid. Being a Top 20 teacher, Mrs. H. prevented this from happening and *kept stupid in the box*.

# REAL EXPERIENCES

Life provides us with real experiences. For example, Paul is sometimes asked to read something and share his opinion. If you gave Paul an article to read, you would not be aware of what was really going on in his head. About a third of the way down the page, Paul would begin thinking, "I'm a slow reader. She thinks I should be done with this by now. I'm feeling stupid." Pretending to have finished reading the entire article, Paul would return it to you and say something like, "Yeah, that's interesting."

People feel stupid when they experience a wide variety of real life situations. Examples of teachers feeling stupid are when they:

**1.** Don't know the answer to a student's question.

**2.** Are confused with computers or technology.

**3.** Forget someone's name.

**4.** Are late for a meeting.

Does it really mean that someone is stupid if he does not know the answer to a question, if she's confused when dealing with technology, if he forgets someone's name, or if she's late for a meeting? Of course not. Then why do we feel stupid when we experience these real situations?

# LETTING STUPID OUT OF THE BOX

Stupid does not exist in reality. What does exist are real experiences such as: not knowing the answer to a student's question, dealing with computers or technology, forgetting someone's name, and being late for a meeting.

Imagine that we carry an Equal Sign in our back pocket. When we experience certain situations, we pull out our equal sign, and place it between the real experience and stupid. It's as if we let stupid out of a box and deem ourselves stupid.

We create the feeling of stupid for ourselves. It wouldn't exist if we didn't equate our real experience to stupid. Without the equal sign, stupid would *stay in the box.*

# FIVE CAUSES OF STUPID

Although *stupid* doesn't exist in reality, it does exist in our thinking. There it can be rampant. For many kids it is the fundamental experience they have in school. John Snobelin, former Canadian Minister of Education, says, "We spend millions of dollars to send kids to school where they come to believe that they are stupid."

We have asked hundreds of students to share with us real situations where they feel stupid and what they do when they feel stupid. Based on their responses, we have identified five causes of stupid or five moments when it is likely for students to pull out their equal sign and judge themselves as stupid. Examples of these are givein for each cause.

## 1. CALLED Many kids experience being called stupid or other words or phrases that mean the same thing. Dumb, idiot, special, retard, and moron are a few of those words.

Student Examples: "When I say something and others say it's stupid or someone says something and I don't know what they mean, they call me stupid and I get mad."

"Every night my dad tells me I'm stupid and I wish I could leave."

This can also occur by being laughed at or by nonverbal expressions or looks. Students identify *that look* from teachers that tells students that they are not getting it.

Obviously we cannot control every word that is spoken in a school or every gesture directed towards a student. However, Top 20 teachers do whatever they can to create a safe environment by having expectations and rules that limit these words from being used and gestures from being expressed.

## 2. COMPARISON Students compare themselves to others or are compared by others.

These comparisons often result in students feeling stupid or Not Good Enough.

Student Examples: "When I am taking standardized tests and am one of the last people taking the test, I rush through it and don't read the questions or answers."

"When some of my friends brag about their grades, I tell them my grades are good then think to myself, 'Oh, I'm stupid.'"

School is a breeding ground for comparisons: grades, honor rolls, making athletic teams or extracurricular activities. It's not that these things should be eliminated from school but that students should be guided so they are not drawing unhealthy conclusions from comparisons.

## 3. CONFUSION A real experience that results in kids feeling stupid is when they are confused, when they don't know or understand something.

Student Examples: "When guys are talking about stats and football and I have no idea what they're talking about, I usually just don't talk or I pretend I know what they are talking about."

"In school when I don't know the answer, I pretend, blush, and don't raise my hand as much."

When we presented the *Mountain of Learning* in Chapter 9, we saw that confusion is a normal and natural condition to learning. However, if kids are feeling stupid when they are confused, we have a major problem. Think of learning as climbing a mountain. Kids who feel stupid when they are confused do not continue on the climb. They quit. They withdraw or stop participating.

Imagine offering a class on learning the alphabet to high school students. If they take that class, they will never be confused and they will all get a high grade. How many students would want to take that class? So many kids would sign up for that class that you'd have standing room only. That's unfortunate because if a student took that class she would learn nothing.

Each day kids walk down hallways in schools until a bell rings. They then go into classrooms. No kid should go into a classroom where he is NOT going to be confused. **If there is no confusion, there is no learning.**

In fact, confusion is the only reason why students should get out of bed in the morning and go to school. They need to go to school because they are confused about reading or math or science or foreign language or small engines or other cultures.

**Top 20 teachers celebrate confusion.** They make confusion part of their curriculum. They restore to confusion the wonderful reputation it ought to have as the moment just before *Aha*. They tap into the natural instinct in children to move through confusion to learning. One way Top 20 teachers do this is by sharing with students their own confusion and helping students realize there is no natural connection between confusion and stupid.

Schools that are worthy of our students' attendance should have a sign outside the front door that says: **CONFUSION ROCKS!!**

## 4. CAN'T
Students frequently feel stupid when they can't do something, when they fail at something or make mistakes.

Student Examples: "When I strike out in a baseball game, I feel that I'm not good at baseball and I'll probably strike out again."

"I tried jumping over a bar on my skate board and didn't make it so I made it look like I did it on purpose."

Like confusion, failure and mistakes have been given a bad reputation. That's unfortunate since all human achievement has been made on the backs of failure and mistakes. Remember, Edison failed many times before he figured out the tungsten filament for the light bulb. Imagine if he had felt stupid after his 428th failure and decided to quit climbing the mountain. Then we'd all still be in the dark.

Kids who develop the belief that they are stupid when they fail can suffer from **the Ooze Factor.** Think of the boy in the first example who said, "When I strike out in a baseball game, I feel that I'm not good at baseball and I'll probably strike out again." If he is thinking this way after he strikes out in the first inning, what is he likely to do at his next at bat? His thinking or belief will make it more likely that he will strike out again in the third inning. **Ooze** means that a negative result in one situation oozes over to cause or influence a bad result in the next situation.

This disease can become more serious. When this occurs, failure in one part of a student's life can negatively impact another part of her life. If she fails a math test and feels stupid, she may perform poorly in her soccer game after school. Performing poorly in her soccer game can result in her expressing angry remarks to her mother and damaging that relationship. Stupid and the ooze factor have taken their toll on many lives.

## 5. CERTAIN SITUATIONS
Students sometimes feel stupid when they find themselves in certain situations. This may occur when they are placed in a certain class, participate in certain activities or need help.

Student Examples: "In any class when I read, I get mad at myself."

"When my hair looks awful, I get stressed and sit there messing with my hair."

"In this class that nobody else takes, I don't let anyone see I'm coming in this room."

Because there are probably students in every school who have this experience, let's take a closer look at this last example. In this particular student's school, all freshmen take algebra or geometry for their math class. This boy was one of fifteen students placed in a pre-algebra class. Just being in that class resulted in his feeling stupid, a feeling that was experienced every day.

> During a visit to this classroom, Paul shared with the students that he has taken many Shakespeare classes, read every Shakespeare play and taught a number of Shakespeare courses. He then asked the students, "If your teacher gave all of us a test on Shakespeare, who do you think would get an A?" The students pointed to Paul.
>
> "Who do you think would get a D or an F?"
>
> All of the students raised their hands.
>
> "What if your teacher gave all of us a test on automobile mechanics. Who would get an F?" Paul raised his hand.
>
> "Who might get an A or a B?" Three boys raised their hands.
>
> "So," asked Paul, "who is stupid? The guy who knows Shakespeare but not automobile mechanics or the boys who know automobile mechanics and not Shakespeare?"
>
> The room got quiet. Nobody raised his or her hand to answer this question. But then a student said, "Neither is stupid. They're just different."

The wisdom from this fourteen-year-old kid needs to be proclaimed across our nation:

**No one is stupid.**
**We are just different.**

Yet countless kids in our schools who are having e: students in this class are not equipped with the same wisdom. They are labeling themselves as stupid. Why is that?

Imagine this circle as representing every thing we could know about life. The wedge in the circle represents school and what typically goes on in school. A long time ago someone decided that a limited number of subjects would be taught in school. These

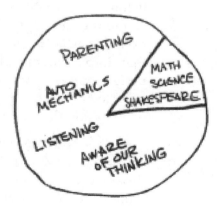

include courses in math, English, science, social studies, and foreign language. If students did well in these and other school-related courses, they were considered to be smart. If they did poorly in these areas, they were considered to be stupid.

But success in life requires awareness, knowledge or skill in many other areas, some of which are more relevant on a daily basis. For example, although Shakespeare may enrich our life, being able to listen well will have a more profound impact on the quality of our life, relationships and learning. Whereas the periodic table might be interesting, being aware of our thinking affects our day-to-day experiences.

We are not suggesting that the current curriculum in our schools ought to be thrown out. What we are suggesting is that, **whatever subjects students take in school, the experience should not result in their believing they are stupid.**

Most schools determine which students are smart. Intentionally or unintentionally, that is unfortunately what commonly occurs in our schools. Wendy Soderman, founder and principal of IDEAL School in Royal Palm Beach, Florida, has created a school that does not determine which kids are smart but *how* kids are smart. During their experience at Ideal School, **all students discover ways in which they are smart.**

That schools should be determining how kids are smart and not which kids are smart is a revolutionary idea that is terribly important. If children do not know how they are smart, *stupid* will have many opportunities to stick to them. But if they know how they are smart, *stupid* has no chance of sticking. These children will live with the wisdom that **"neither is stupid…they're different."**

Because Top 20 teachers are aware of this wisdom, their students have a better chance of discovering it for themselves.

Before we leave this section on the causes of stupid, we need to realize that stupid is experienced by students across the spectrum of academic success, from low achievers to high achievers. This is evidenced by a girl who said that she feels stupid when she gets 99% on a test. Why is that? She's not perfect, but her family culture might make her think that that is what is expected of her. Imagine the potential danger for students who believe that nothing short of perfection can demonstrate their intelligence.

Then there's the student who feels stupid when he's the first one done taking a test. Why? Being the first one done means he's a nerd, a whole different way of feeling socially stupid. This is a good reminder to adults who work with youth that feelings of stupid are not limited to academic or intellectual areas of their lives but extend to social and all others areas of their lives as well.

# REACTIONS TO FEELING STUPID

What do students do when they feel stupid? Students have expressed a wide array of reactions to feelings of stupid that fall into eight categories.

1. **Withdraw:** Some students back away from experiences both in and out of school. They quit school or quit participating in school. They won't try things that might be challenging. They won't try out for athletic teams or other co-curricular activities. They get quiet. They no longer raise their hand to ask questions or share ideas during discussion times.

2. **Pretend:** They fake responses so that their stupidity is not detected by others.

3. **React Emotionally:** They feel embarrassed, angry, upset, sad, worried, nervous, or stressed.

4. **Judge**: They frequently make self-limiting judgments about themselves: "I'm not good enough," "I don't know anything, " "I'm bad at everything," "I'm stupid."

5. **Act Out:** They misbehave in class or on the playground. They lash out at others by arguing, swearing, fighting, challenging or bullying.

6. **Become Defensive:** They defend themselves by judging their classes or teachers: "This class is stupid. When am I ever going to need this? My teacher's stupid."

7. **Become Motivated:** They sometimes work harder or study more in order to do better. This appears to have positive results because they may do better on the next test. However, we shouldn't be fooled by the external results. Being stupid is still attached to their sense of self. We don't want kids to study because they have feelings of stupid. We want them to study because they are curious and have a real desire to learn.

8. **Become Numb:** Some students believe that being numb is better than dumb. Apathy is one form of numb: "I don't care. Whatever." Another dangerous means of becoming numb in teenagers is drugs and alcohol. A student who feels stupid in school Monday through Friday might be looking to feel numb once she leaves school for the weekend.

# TOP 20 TEACHERS ARE AWARE OF STUPID

**T**RUE
**T**ALES

Stu Wiley, principal of York Elementary School in York, Nebraska, attended our presentation *Roadblock to Success: I Am Stupid* at the National Association of Elementary School Principals Conference. Ironically, Stu was actually looking for a different presentation when he accidentally wandered into our room.

Upon returning to his school after the conference, he was informed by the kindergarten teacher that one of her students had been acting out and disturbing the class. After meeting with the child, Mr. Wiley sent us the following email.

"I appreciated your presentation at NAESP in Nashville, and wanted to let you know one of my kindergarten students has turned around his misbehavior since we talked about how he felt stupid in the classroom. Thank you!!"

This is a story with a happy ending. However, imagine if Mr. Wiley had not accidentally heard this session on stupid. How do principals usually deal with misbehaving students? It's possible the child would have received some form of discipline. Would that have solved the problem? Probably not. But because this principal was aware of what might have really been going on in this child, he was able to effectively handle this situation.

What is disturbing about this story is that this child is in kindergarten. Already, at such an early age, this student is having significant feelings of being stupid. Imagine what his school experience would be like in his future if he hadn't experienced a Top 20 principal who was aware of the power of stupid and helped him get stupid back in the box. Every child needs to meet adults like this in a place called school.

Stupid has had a devastating effect on the lives and learning of American youth. Its power to minimize the potential of our students is staggering. If we are to overcome this damaging impact, our entire teaching profession needs to become aware that stupid is loose in our schools. If we remain unaware of this reality, children will continue to be victimized. But if we, as a profession, engage in serious discussions about how stupid is impacting our students, we will find ways to minimize its negative affect and get stupid back in the box.

Although each individual teacher and faculty needs to determine their own strategies, the following suggestions may be helpful.

1. Make *stupid* a part of the curriculum. As teachers we can talk about stupid with our students. We can share situations in which we experience feelings of stupid.

2. Help parents become aware of *stupid* and its causes.

3. Use the Equal Sign. Give each student an equal sign and post a large equal sign on the classroom wall. When situations arise where *stupid* is likely to appear, ask the students if any of them have pulled out their equal sign. For example, after returning a test, ask the class if any felt stupid while taking the test or now when they are getting the results.

4. Help students discover how they are smart. Translate the multiple intelligences into language the students can understand and help them identify their strengths. Have them state specific ways in which they are smart: "I am smart. I am good at _____."

5. Have each student fill in the blanks for himself and then have all students repeat each sentence in unison:

   "I am smart. I am just confused about _____."
   "I am smart. I just can't _____ yet."

6. Be on the look out for *stupid*. Discuss with students situations in their lives where stupid is likely to arise. Discuss with other professionals aspects of school culture, traditions and practices that encourage *stupid* to come out of the box.

7. Check-ins: Identify ways of measuring in individual students and in the school as a whole if *stupid* is growing stronger or weaker.

Imagine the learning that would go on in a school where mistakes and confusion are celebrated and stupid is kept in the box. Top 20 teachers carry keys that open doors to curiosity and lock away roadblocks to learning.

# TIME FOR REFLECTION & ACTION

1. What are situations in which you feel stupid? How do you react when you feel stupid?

2. What causes of stupid do you see in your classroom and school? How can you remove these causes for your students?

3. What did you become aware of while reading this chapter regarding an action you would like to take? What action would you like to take?

# CHAPTER 11

## TOP 20 TEACHERS

# Stop the Spread of Negativity in Themselves and Their School

Walking into the teachers' lounge, Barb sees three other teachers sitting around the table that she has been eating at since she was hired eight years ago. As she sets down her lunch, she throws a packet of papers in the center of the table and says in an angry tone, "Did you see this? It's the benefits package for next school year. You have got to be kidding me! It's far worse than last year!"

Simon, a veteran social studies teacher, chimes in, "It's as if there is no respect for those of us who have given our whole lives to this place!  After 30 years here I  can't even get dental insurance that covers fillings!"

Karen, the most popular teacher in the building, attempts to top both Barb and Simon by throwing in her two cents, "At the school I used to be at, they had the best insurance coverage ever. I didn't have to pay a dime. Now that's the way every school should be run!"

The conversation continued as each teacher dumped more negativity. Greg, the new teacher at the end of the table, contributed his own negative comments even though he was excited to have a paying job and any sort of benefits. He realized quickly that the rules of this game were that he better complain too if he didn't want to be thrown out of the group. Although he entered the lunch hour feeling Above the Line, he left depressed and cynical about his employer and his job.

Barb caught her breath after the other three teachers left the table. She suddenly became aware that her Thursday was slipping away from her, that the negativity swirling around the table had polluted the only thirty-minute break during her hectic day. "I'm going to look at this differently," she reminded herself, "and tomorrow I am not going to let my day get thrashed."

# TORNADOES

What occurred in this faculty lounge is a Tornado, a Below the Line habit that many teachers participate in daily. **A social Tornado is powerful negative energy that pulls all involved farther and farther Below the Line.** Just like an actual twister, a BTL Tornado will destroy anything in its path.

Tornadoes are attempts to bond in misery by influencing others to agree on how bad things are. They are very different from a group of people discussing a negative situation intending to problem solve and having everyone's best interest in mind.

Although Tornadoes occur in most workplaces, their chronic negativity is particularly alarming for those who work in schools. Teaching is difficult and exhausting. Feeling overwhelmed, we often spew out negativity every time we gather with fellow educators. This behavior does nothing to keep ourselves emotionally healthy. We all have Below the Line moments. However, when teachers become chronically negative, we then become toxic to our students. **Children CANNOT flourish around adults who are chronically negative!**

Top 20 teachers avoid chronic negativity by being conscious of Tornado Watches, Warnings and Touchdowns.

**Tornado Watch:** Being aware of when the conditions are right to likely spawn a Tornado. For teachers, some of these may include:

- Faculty and department meetings
- Lunch hours
- Happy hours or staff social events
- Co-curricular activities
- Times of change
- Parent conferences
- Announcements of salary and benefits package

Being aware of these potential Tornado inciting conditions, Top 20 teachers are better able to identify Tornadoes and protect themselves from their harmful energy.

**Tornado Warning:** A Tornado has been spotted! A sure warning occurs when something negative is said about someone who is not present. Once aware of a Tornado's presence, Top 20 teachers make a conscious choice about how best to handle it:

**99**

1. Avoid the chaos altogether and spend time with those people who are also attempting to live Above the Line. Although there may be social consequences to doing so, Top 20 teachers know that taking care of their emotional health is more important than being popular with the negative crowd.

2. When someone attempts to start a Tornado by complaining, Top 20 teachers respond to the complaint by simply saying, "Okay" or "I hear you." These responses reveal that we are listening, but choosing not to throw more gas on the fire. We are avoiding the tendency to tell our own negative story in an effort to show solidarity with the complainer. By staying Above the Line, we are more helpful to colleagues who are Below the Line than if we were to dive Below with them.

3. Purposefully start conversations that are about positive topics: "We only have 25 minutes for lunch. Let's talk about something more fun than disrespectful students. What is everybody doing this weekend?"

**Tornado Touchdown:** A touchdown occurs when we join the Below the Line party and contribute some negativity ourselves. However, having participated in the Tornado doesn't mean we have to continue. Realizing that we have been negative, we can choose one of the steps above to end the situation. We can acknowledge to the group that we wish we hadn't gotten caught up in the drama and apologize for anything we wish we hadn't said.

> Example: "You know, I'm just being negative. I'm sorry about what I just said. I'd rather that we spend our time together talking about something more positive. Anybody doing anything interesting during spring break?"

## TORNADO STARTER

**TRUE TALES**

Now that she is aware of Tornadoes, Willow realizes that she had not only been a participant in many Tornadoes, but was actually a Tornado Starter. When she had the good gossip or started a negative conversation that was then supported by others, she felt powerful and popular. After realizing that she was pulling others Below the Line and ruining her own day, she made a conscious choice to no longer be popular in that way. No magic wand was waived that took all negativity out of Willow's life. However, by being more positive in her interactions with others, she has attracted more positive people into her social circle.

## THOUGHT CIRCLES

While checking her mailbox, Miss Chang found a note from her principal: "Kim, see me." Going immediately Below the Line, Miss Chang began an anxiety-filled chain of thoughts: "What does he want to talk to me about? I wonder if my department chairperson told him that I missed the meeting last week…She's a thorn in my side…I miss one meeting and she tattles on me…I'll tell him how bad of a department chair she is…I give this job my all, stay late, show up earlier than all the other teachers and I get in trouble… This is so unfair…I'll just quit…I don't need this kind of STRESS!"

Although Miss Chang wasn't aware of it, she was creating an alternative reality in which she was going further and further Below the Line. After this internal negative spiraling, she stomped into the principal's office and announced, "You know what? Mrs. Thompson is a nutcase. So I skipped last week's meeting. It's not like we ever get anything done with her as the Chair. I'm so fed up with this place. I quit!"

Perplexed by her response, her principal responded, "Really, Kim? I asked you to see me because I nominated you for Teacher of the Month. But tell me more about the meeting you skipped."

Tornadoes are not the only sort of negativity in schools that need to be managed. Our own negative thinking can muddy the waters of our lives. Thought Circles are Below the Line mental habits that, if gone unchecked, can pollute our lives with anxiety, worry, frustration and anger.

Thought Circles occur when a thought about a piece of factual information steamrolls Below the Line picking up more and more negative possibilities along the way. The result of this collection of negative thoughts, which may or may not be logically connected to each other, is that our thinking gets distorted and unclear. Any decision, like Miss Chang's, made under this mental condition is likely to create a mess.

## PUTTING AN END TO THOUGHT CIRCLES

The longer a Thought Circle lasts the more it will contaminate our lives. The first step in nipping a Thought Circle in the bud is to be aware we are having one. Once aware, we can then say to ourselves, "Let the problem be the problem." Although we commonly make any situation worse by imagining more dire outcomes, by *letting the problem be the problem* we change our Frame and see the situation differently. Kim could have

**101**

avoided a miserable experience had she simply thought, "My boss wants to see me. The only problem I have is that I have to go to his office before I go home." By seeing it this way, Kim would have approached her boss differently and had a much more pleasant experience.

## NOT NOW AND PARKING LOT

Two other ways to manage Thought Circles are to use **Not Now** and **Parking Lot.** When we catch ourselves having Thought Circles, we can say, "Stop. This is a Thought Circle. It's not in my best interest. NOT NOW!" This prevents the Thought Circle from picking up steam and pulling us further Below the Line.

Sometimes the concern that is the origin of a Thought Circle does need to be seriously considered. When we are unable to give a problem or situation the attention it may require at the time, we can put that issue in our mental Parking Lot until later when we have time to deal with it. This allows us to focus on the present and get through the day. Because we are not spending the entire day Below the Line and our thinking will be clearer, we will handle the situation more effectively and make a better decision.

Top 20 teachers avoid burnout and chronic negativity. They are aware that negative thinking and divisive social behaviors prevent teachers and students from achieving their true potential. Negativity keeps schools stuck in dysfunctional cycles. Top 20 teachers create a healthy work environment and school culture by reducing Tornadoes and Thought Circles. In doing so, they also model positive self-skills for their students.

# TIME FOR REFLECTION & ACTION

1. Where do you encounter Tornadoes as a teacher?

2. What is the effect Tornadoes have on you or others in your school?

3. What can you do to reduce the damaging impact of Tornadoes?

4. Are there situations around which you commonly experience Thought Circles?

5. What did you become aware of while reading this chapter regarding an action you would like to take? What action would you like to take?

# CHAPTER 12

## TOP 20 TEACHERS
# Resolve Conflicts Effectively

The guest presenter that Sarah Jones had invited to speak about Martin Luther King's philosophy of nonviolence to her third and fourth period social studies classes had requested that the sessions be held in the school's auditorium. When she went to reserve the auditorium, she noticed that John Wilcox, who taught the same kids she did, had already reserved that space for his third hour English class. Her first thought was to see her department head and complain about the frequent use of the auditorium by the English department.

On her way to her department head's office, she thought, "Wait a second…this is silly. There's got to be a better way of handling this." Needing a place to think, she stepped into the women's restroom. She felt the anxiety that always bubbled up in her whenever she experienced conflict and recounted several times when she avoided dealing with these situations. "I'm tired of being this way," she thought. "I need to see this differently."

As she approached John's classroom, she hoped she would find him alone. "John," she said, addressing her colleague, "do you have a few moments to chat?"

"Sure," he said. "What's up?"

"I noticed you're using the auditorium third period on Thursday."

"Yes," he responded, "and fourth period on Friday."

"May I ask what you need it for?"

"I want the kids to watch a gang scene from *West Side Story* on the video screen. Then I'm going to give them an assignment to work on in small groups."

"Let me share with you my problem," said Sarah.

Their conversation continued for another five minutes when John said, "I have an idea. What if we combined our classes? During third period, both groups could hear the talk on Dr. King and during fourth hour I could do my lesson and assignment. That way I'd only have to do it once. Besides, there might be something your speaker talks about that will connect with the gang scene from *West Side Story*. Would you mind helping me manage the kids during fourth period?"

"Not at all," said Sarah. "Sounds like a great idea. Thanks, John. See you on Thursday."

With life comes conflict. Whether between individuals, groups or nations, people struggle with each other to get what is important to them. Some conflicts, like Sarah's, create a bit of anxiety but don't have a major impact on our life adventure. Other conflicts take a more serious toll as they destroy dreams, relationships and lives. Is destruction, small or large, a natural part of conflict or is some more desirable outcome possible?

## CONFLICT IN THE FRAME

How we think about and respond to conflict has a major impact on our lives, relationships and experiences. Having asked thousands of people how they see conflict in their Frame, we now understand how most people commonly feel, what they do and what they get.

How we **SEE** conflict: a threat, danger, an adversarial disagreement, battle, struggle, controversy, Win-Lose. The issue is more important than the relationship with the other person.

How we **FEEL:** anxious, angry, fearful, frustrated, stressed, worried, doubtful, inadequate, hopeless, tense, need to be right.

What we **DO:** fight, argue, withdraw, avoid, yell, blame, lash out, defend, attack, interrupt, judge, cry.

What we **GET:** nothing, hurt feelings, damaged relationships, stress, mistrust, bigger problems, more conflict.

This is not only how many of us see conflict, it is also what we have *practiced* for many years. As a result, we have gotten quite good at experiencing conflict this way. It has become a habit.

If this is what conflict is all about, it is understandable why we would want to avoid it. Unfortunately, no matter what we may want, life keeps offering us conflict opportunities.

# TOE-TO-TOE CONFLICT

The best way to describe this experience of conflict is Toe-to-Toe. It's like two boxers facing each other Toe-to-Toe. When the bell rings, they begin wailing on each other and hope to make the other bloody. One seeks to win at the expense of the other's loss.

Let's consider how Sarah would have handled the situation with John in a Toe-to-Toe fashion.

**SEE:** She sees him as an adversary who is blocking her from getting what she wants. If he gets the auditorium during third hour, he wins and she loses. If she wants to win, she needs to make him give up the auditorium during that time.

**FEEL:** The conflict makes her tense. She is frustrated because this is so unfair that the English department overuses the auditorium. She feels disrespected and is embarrassed to call the guest speaker about not having the desired space. She is Below the Line and her thinking is neither clear nor in her best interest.

**DO:** She either avoids dealing with this altogether, dumps it on her department head or marches into John's room. With her Below the Line thinking, she makes judgments about his selfishness and arrogance, blames him for her problem, plans what she is going to say while he is talking and interrupts him frequently.

**GET:** She gets a colleague who is upset with her and no auditorium for her guest speaker. She gets more tension and stress as she regrets the way she handles the situation. She buries the problem alive only to be reminded that she has taken a withdrawal from her trust account with John when they pass in the hall the next day and he looks the other way.

# INEFFECTIVE ROLES

Because we have often *practiced* Toe-to-Toe, we may have developed roles that we easily take on whenever we engage in a conflict situation. The following Toe-to-Toe roles will keep us in the battle and increase the intensity of the conflict.

**Historian** (a teacher speaking to a student): "I remember you turning in a late homework assignment six months ago. It was October 12th and you promised to never miss another assignment after that one." When we are in this role, we bring up things from the past in order to prove our point. What happened months or years ago is never over to a historian.

**Lawyer** (a teacher speaking to a parent): "No, you did not ask me to call you if your son got a C grade. You asked me to call if I was *worried* about his grades. I specifically took note of your request. My teaching partner could verify that." When we are in the lawyer role, we look for loopholes and provide evidence and witnesses.

**Doormat** (a teacher responding to a department head's request to change teaching methods): "Oh, okay, I guess I'll just do it your way. After all, I have only been in the classroom for twenty-three years, so I am sure that I don't know how to teach." In the doormat role we are apathetic and go along with whatever someone is saying. We might do this just so they will leave us alone, and then we go back to operating our old way.

**Sarcastic Tone** (a teacher speaking to a student): "Oh, was this test h-a-a-r-r-r-d? It must be very h-a-a-r-r-r-d to be a high school student these days. Was your limousine late picking you up for school this morning?" We can also use tone to dominate or make someone feel stupid.

**Grammar Teacher** (a teacher responding to a parent): "You are telling me that 'me and my daughter' will be coming in to talk about her behavior. Actually, it should be 'my daughter and I.' If you cannot even use proper English then I don't know how we'll ever solve her problems." Using the role of grammar teacher allows us to avoid dealing with the real issue.

**Intellectual** (a teacher speaking to a student): "I will look at your essay again, but I am certain that it was graded correctly. I was *summa cum laude* at Harvard and am the head of the department." The intellectual comes off as a know-it-all who cannot be challenged.

These are only a few of the many roles we can adapt when we get into conflict situations. If we are unaware of these, we will continue to deal with conflict in ineffective ways.

# BUTTON PUSHING

Probably the most ineffective response to conflict is **button pushing.** In using this strategy, we determine a sensitive and important issue for the other person and attack it. John could have pushed Sarah's button by saying, "You try to make yourself look good by bringing in someone to talk about Dr. King, but you always have to have things your way." John would not only be disagreeing with Sarah but hurting her deeply by touching on her insecurities.

Button pushing certainly prevents any sort of resolution from taking place. More importantly, the hurt that it causes will significantly damage the relationship and linger for a long time in a person's emotional memory bank. As such, it offers an invitation for revenge.

## DISCOVERY PARTY

Most of us have experienced conflict as an invitation to a Below the Line party. Once we RSVP to this party, it becomes a BYON affair – Bring Your Own Negativity. Since others who come to the party tend to do the same thing, the party becomes quite negative. Because this has been our common experience, we expect this same result whenever a conflict pops up in our life. With that experience and expectation, we are likely to handle the next conflict Toe-to-Toe.

Top 20s, however, know that another option exists. They view conflict not as an invitation to a Below the Line party but as **an invitation to a Discovery Party.** They see conflict as an opportunity to discover something beneficial if they BYOV and BYOC.

**BYOV means Bring Your Own Values.** Top 20s come to the party knowing what is important to them. They are aware of the values they want to communicate and the way they want to act during the interaction.

**BYOC means Bring Your Own Curiosity.** Because Top 20s bring curiosity to the party, they listen and discover what is important to the other person. Their curiosity also enables them to discover ways by which they and the other person can attain their desired results. Furthermore, by being curious, they sometimes discover a third possibility other than *my way* and *your way* that may provide greater results for everyone. This happened in the conflict between Sarah and John.

## HEART-TO-HEART CONFLICT RESOLUTION

By seeing conflict as an invitation to a Discovery Party, Top 20s approach the situation Heart-to-Heart.

How Top 20s **SEE** conflict: a Win-Win opportunity, as mutually benefi-cial, a partnership. The issue and the relationship are both important.

How Top 20s **FEEL**: excited, hopeful, willing, cooperative, open, optimistic.

What Top 20s **DO**: listen to understand, ask questions, contribute ideas, respect all involved, encourage, communicate desire to find mutually beneficial solutions.

What Top 20s **GET**: satisfactory resolution, stronger relationship, greater trust, respect.

Practicing Heart-to-Heart does not assure that we will get the results we desire. However, it does result in two tremendous outcomes. First, when we practice Heart-to-Heart, we maintain our self-respect. We cannot control other people, but we can act in ways that are consistent with our own values. We can be the way we want to be. That is a very important outcome in our encounters with people. On the other hand, by going Toe-to-Toe we often give up our self-respect. We say things we wish we hadn't said and respond in ways that leave us with regret.

A second outcome of Heart-to-Heart is how it affects *next time*. It's likely that we will have future conflicts with this same person. If we have handled a previous situation with this person in a Toe-to-Toe fashion, it is unlikely that we will have a mutually beneficial resolution the *next time*. Because of the low trust between us and the negative experience we have shared, it is likely that our next encounter will bring more of the same. However, the trust, respect and cooperation that are communicated when we practice Heart-to-Heart set a positive foundation for a highly successful experience *next time*.

Furthermore, by practicing Heart-to-Heart we get better at it. As it becomes habitual, it influences the reputation others will have of us. They may even come to believe that when they engage in a conflict with us that **they cannot lose.** If that is our reputation, incredible possibilities lay ahead.

## 'YOU' STATEMENTS AND 'I' STATEMENTS

The manner by which we address people has a major impact on whether or not we handle conflicts effectively. Conflicts are made worse when people feel blamed or accused. A primary way this happens is when *you* statements are used. *You* statements tend to point the finger at the other person.

"You always need to have it your way."

"You arrange the class schedule to benefit youself."

The conflict can be better managed by using *I* statements. *I* statements take the focus off what we think the other person has done to us and reduces our tendency to blame. They help us identify our own feelings and, as a result, elicit a less defensive response from the other person.

*I* statements typically follow the pattern: "I feel _____ when _____."

"I feel discounted when my ideas are not considered."

"I feel it's unfair the way the class schedule has been arranged."

If we can keep the channels of communication open during conflict situations, we have a better chance of coming to resolution. *I* statements are more likely to keep those channels open.

# PARTNERS, NOT ADVERSARIES

Another major impact in a conflict situation is how we see the other person. Usually we view the other person as being on the opposite side of the issue. We see her as an opponent or adversary. In fact, as the picture suggests, when we think of the problem, we can easily think of the other person as **being** the problem. After all, if it weren't for this person and her point of view, we wouldn't have a problem. If she just got out of the way, everything would be fine.

Seeing the other person this way often prevents us from discovering a satisfactory solution. Rather, it tends to make the problem worse and last longer.

It is much more effective in resolving conflict for the people involved to see each other as partners working together to discover something mutually beneficial. Rather than facing each other with the problem in between, they are standing side by side and looking at the problem. By using an item that they are both looking at to represent the problem, they are more likely to see **the problem** as the problem and not **the other person** as the problem.

As they examine the problem from this point of view, they share what is important to each other and what each other needs (BYOV). Knowing the results each wants to attain, they work together to see if they can find a solution that will achieve those results. By responding to the conflict in a Heart-to-Heart manner, they are more likely not only to discover a mutually satisfying solution but also to build trust and strengthen their relationship.

## PRACTICE AND PREPARATION

If we are in the habit of responding to conflict in a Toe-to-Toe manner, it is because we have practiced this way many times. If we are to change to a Heart-to-Heart manner, we have to practice as well. One way of doing this is simply to visualize ourselves responding in a Heart-to-Heart way. By imagining what we would say and do in a particular situation, we are more likely to carry that out in action.

Preparation prior to engaging in the conflict situation is also critically important. Imagine a team about to participate in an athletic competition. For thirty or more minutes before the game begins, the athletes warm up, stretch and practice the skills that will help them succeed. They are also getting mentally prepared for the contest.

We need to make similar preparations if we want a successful outcome from a conflict. By focusing on the following areas, we can prepare ourselves for a more successful experience:

1. Identify what is important to us.

2. Commit to listening to understand what the other person needs and what is important to him. We never create problems by listening. We often create problems or make them worse by not listening.

3. See the other person as a partner in discovering what would be mutually beneficial. Prepare to tell the other person that we want to work cooperatively to find the best solution for each other.

4. If necessary, practice *I* statements.

Practice and preparation don't make perfect, but they do make better. Furthermore, they will help us develop a habit of responding to conflict Heart-to-Heart.

# TIME FOR REFLECTION & ACTION

1. Use the Frame to examine recent conflicts you have had:

   A. How did you see the conflict?

   B. What were your feelings?

   C. What did you do?

   D. What were the results?

2. Which of the six Toe-to-Toe roles (p. 106) are ways you respond in conflict situations? Are there other roles that you commonly take on when dealing with conflict?

3. Think of a conflict you have experienced or are experiencing.

   BYOV: A. What do you want from this issue that is important to you?

   B. How do you want to behave during this conflict?

   BYOC: A. How can you use curiosity to discover what's important to the other person?

   B. How can you use curiosity to discover what's mutually beneficial for both of you?

4. Create your own preparation strategy that you will use prior to dealing with a conflict situation.

5. What did you become aware of while reading this chapter regarding an action you would like to take? What action would you like to take?

# CHAPTER 13

## Top 20 Teachers
# Are Aware of What Gets Activated in Them

Mrs. Martinez was returning the test papers to her seventh grade science class. While correcting the tests the evening before, she grew frustrated. Each test seemed worse than the previous one. Now, she was struggling to control her temper as the volume in the classroom escalated. She could detect an undercurrent of negative comments about the returned exams. "Stop it," she demanded with her blood boiling. "Settle down right this minute! We'll go over these tests just as soon as everyone is ready to begin. Now what in the world happened on this test yesterday?"

The students shuffled in their seats nervously. Mrs. Martinez paused during the awkward silence, collected herself and took a deep Top 20 breath. "Let's start over," she offered. "I think I know what the problem is now. Help me understand the parts of this test you are still confused about. Raise your hand if you have an insight about what happened yesterday."

Before becoming fully aware of what was really happening in her classroom that afternoon, Mrs. Martinez was on the verge of creating a disaster. Fortunately for her and her students, her high EQ kicked in and she caught herself just in the nick of time. Being aware of herself, she realized that the confrontation had more to do with her than with her students. Once aware of that, she avoided the negative incident and the atmosphere in the room became safe again.

In earlier chapters, we focused on topics like the Line, Invitations, Indicators and Messages. Now we will use these concepts to combat the worst moments that happen in the classroom. Throughout the school year, several random teacher Invitations are sent our way. These negative events are part of the territory. When we are unaware of what's really getting activated in us, we are unable to deal effectively with these Invitations in a Top 20 manner.

# ACTIVATING 'NOT GOOD ENOUGH'

Let's take a look at what was really going on in Mrs. Martinez' situation. While correcting the exams the previous evening, the first Invitation she received was poor test results. A common teacher response to such an Invitation is to blame: "They don't work hard enough," or "They don't care enough about their own education," or "Their parents aren't supervising homework time." However, our blame may be the outward manifestation of what is unconsciously being activated in us: "If I were a better teacher, then these students would be succeeding." The message Mrs. Martinez may have actually heard from the low test scores was about herself, "You are not good enough." Had she detected this in the moment, she would have seen these Not Good Enough messages clearly:

- "The students failed because you did not teach them."
- "You are not good enough as a teacher."
- "Someone will find out about this."

These messages activated in Mrs. Martinez an NGE belief about herself. As she passed out the tests the next day and the students became disruptive, more NGE messages were sent her way. Although this was really happening within her, she was unaware of it. Her Below the Line Indicators included feelings of helplessness and anger and resulted in a louder and more negative tone in her voice.

A variety of situations tend to set off teachers' negative Indicators. Some of these random Invitations occur when:

- Classroom disruptions happen.
- Poor test scores occur.
- Student apathy shows up.
- Students are called out of class for other appointments.
- Negative parental emails or comments come our way.
- Other teachers succeed or receive awards.
- The administration ignores our input.

Remember, each of these is simply an Invitation that we choose to accept or turn down. On the surface, these Invitations appear to be sure-fire Below the Line moments. The anatomy of what happens next is crucial. Once Below the Line,

our thinking becomes unclear, our Indicators turn on and we tend to make bad decisions. These BTL decisions rarely improve the situation and usually make it worse. Occasionally, these situations erupt into even more damaging incidents.

Some of the most confrontational and negative situations in our career have come as a result of how we have handled random Invitations. When students are apathetic about their learning, it is easy to make the leap to judgment: "They are doing this because I am not good enough." When a student is taken out of our class for a counselor's appointment, it is easy to believe: "They think my class is not valuable."

Tom had been teaching math in grade school and high school for over thirty-five years. Three years ago he had an insight about a seemingly harmless practice that he had been using since 1974. After every chapter exam, he would post the Top Ten test grades on the classroom wall. He would then mention those outstanding scores aloud to the class the day after the test, lauding those who had achieved these superior results.

## TOP 10

| | | | |
|---|---|---|---|
| Anderson | 101 | O'Malley | 96 |
| Sanchez | 98 | Smith | 96 |
| Becker | 98 | Lepinski | 94 |
| Yang | 97 | Carpenter | 94 |
| Collins | 96 | Martin | 93 |

On the surface, it seemed like he was going out of his way to congratulate deserving students. Digging deeper, he discovered what was really taking place. He would point out the top scores in an attempt to get across two things to the class. First, he wanted them all to know that those top scores proved that he was, indeed, doing an outstanding job in teaching the material. Next, he wanted everyone to know that had they applied themselves adequately, they, would also be featured on the Top Ten list.

Tom's realization ironically occurred when he was presenting a Top 20 seminar to a group of teachers. One of the teachers shared how a local middle school conducted its academic awards ceremony every spring. An all-school assembly would be held in the auditorium where the ten students with the best grades would be called to the stage. They were given pizza to eat in front of the other 900 students as a reward for their outstanding work in class. Tom saw this as detrimental to students and, seeing the connection with his Top Ten list, abandoned this practice. Now he simply jots a note of congratulations on the bottom of those A+ tests.

## TEACHERS' INDICATORS

We all have our favorite dysfunctional behaviors that come out when we go Below the Line. A few that have been detected include:

- Being sarcastic
- Threatening punishments
- Yelling

- Making negative judgments
- Blaming or using guilt
- Being apathetic, shutting down, withdrawing

Some teachers lower their standards when students struggle. An easy test eliminates the teacher's NGE feeling. Other teachers respond to poor test scores with the opposite approach. They raise standards, hoping to show the class just who's in charge. None of these responses are effective. Most of these Indicators serve to make the situations even worse.

## BECOMING AWARE OF OUR POWER TO MAKE CHOICES

We can only make choices when we become aware that we have the power to make choices. In the heat of the moment, we often simply react instantly to these negative situations. Since we are reacting with little or no time to collect ourselves, the responses tend to lack clarity, good judgment and effectiveness.

If so, then what's the formula for success? How can we survive and thrive in these difficult situations? When we receive a *hit,* an unexpected negative event, and go Below the Line, our reaction is immediate and usually ineffective. When we are Above the Line and aware of our thinking, an elegant pause comes between the *hit* and the response.

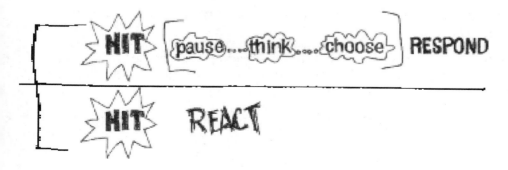

If we are able to pause, even for the briefest moment, we allow ourselves to insert our value into the situation: "I do not belittle children," or "I will remain in control," or "I will hang onto my positive day." Below the Line thinking blurs awareness of our value. Consequently, we often act contrary to our value.

Unfortunately, we cannot change if we remain unaware that we are Below the Line and may need to go through three steps on the road to Top 20 awareness and recovery:

Step 1: We become aware **after** the incident is over: "Wow, I didn't handle that parent call very well. I got scared and reacted without pausing. No wonder things got messy."

Step 2: We become aware **during** the incident itself: "Wow, I am yelling at a sixth-grader. This is an NGE message getting to me and I've gone Below the Line. Sorry, sixth-grader, my bad."

Step 3: We become aware on the front end **when the Invitation arrives:** "Wow, four kids just came to class late and I have two parent phone calls to return. I'd better watch my thinking closely right now."

Top 20 teachers are aware of what's really going on in their classrooms. Sometimes that awareness includes the ability to look in the mirror to see the power they have to make choices that create a positive difference for everyone involved.

# TIME FOR REFLECTION & ACTION

1. What Invitations do you receive and accept as a teacher? (See examples on p. 113.)

2. Regarding these Invitations, what are your Indicators when you go Below the Line?

3. Is there a connection between these Indicators and feelings that you are Not Good Enough?

4. Identify values you have that you want to stay aware of when you take a *hit*.

5. What did you become aware of while reading this chapter regarding an action you would like to take? What action would you like to take?

# CHAPTER 14

# Top 20 Teachers
# Practice Kaizen

A mother came to Mahatma Gandhi concerned about how much sugar her son was eating. She asked the great leader if he would talk to her son about eating too much sugar. Gandhi asked the mother to come back in a week. When the mother returned the following week, Gandhi agreed to speak to her son. The mother asked Gandhi, "Why couldn't you have told my son last week to stop eating sugar?" Gandhi replied, "Last week I was eating sugar. This week I gave it up."

The principle presented in this simple story is the central tenet of Gandhi's leadership philosophy: "We must be the change we wish to see in the world."

Teachers must be authentic. It is only by being true to our core values and purpose that we can inspire our students. For Top 20 teachers, a fundamental value and purpose is the philosophy of **kaizen**. Kaizen refers to **continuous improvement throughout all aspects of life.** A Japanese word, kaizen consists of *kai,* which means change, and *zen,* which mean good.

The mother wanted Gandhi to bring about *good change* in her son. The purpose of teaching is to bring about good change in our students. We want our students to grow and to experience continual improvement. For this to happen, "we must be the change we wish to see" in our students.

- If we want curiosity to stay alive in our students, we must overcome our need to be right and stay curious.

- If we want students to move outside their Comfort Zone and learn from mistakes, we must be willing to attempt new things outside of our Comfort Zones and learn from our mistakes.

- If we want our students to listen, we must be active listeners.

- If we want students to develop Star Qualities through school, we must develop our own Star Qualities through teaching.

- If we want students to overcome limiting beliefs and keep stupid in the box, we must deal with our own limiting beliefs and feelings of stupid.

Top 20 teachers passionately practice kaizen. They desire to grow and learn more about their students, their profession and themselves. The following are examples of the passion for kaizen in educators at the end and beginning of their careers.

## A VETERAN'S KAIZEN

School provides a routine. Classes begin and end at regular times. The schedule of events is pretty much the same year to year. After many years of teaching, the experience of a school year can become banal and mundane. It's easy as the years rush by to get stuck in mediocrity and be tempted to just sit back and ride out the rest of a career until retirement: "It's easiest to just do the same thing over and over. I don't want to rock the boat. I'll stay invisible until that magic date when I can get out of here!" In the midst of this temptation, Top 20 teachers instead maintain a desire for growth and continual improvement.

Even though she was only two years away from retirement, Pat Heird jumped at the opportunity to attend a Top 20 session. After attending the three-day training, Pat returned to her home in Windsor, Colorado, committed to implementing what she had learned into her own life. When school began the next fall, she used Top 20 concepts with the students in her role as the school's counselor.

"I'm really enjoying teaching Top 20 to groups of eighth graders at our middle school," wrote Pat. "Top 20 has offered me new insight into counseling students, their parents, and our staff. Since starting our program, I've watched kids' light bulbs turn on over and over again as they become aware of the choices they are making to create happy and successful lives for themselves. This is the best ride I've had in 36 years in education and my students are enjoying the ride, too!"

Pat's personal kaizen made a positive difference in her students' lives as she began to teach Top 20 classes in her school. Her classes included students with a wide range of social and academic ability levels. One student, who will be called Todd, was dealing with behavioral difficulties.

"Our last day of class was the Friday before Christmas vacation. I had visited with Todd twice that day regarding a conflict he had with a teacher. When I got home after school, the assistant principal called to tell me Todd had returned to school to see me. The AP said he seemed quite agitated but left when I wasn't there. I was well aware that Todd had not been taking his bi-polar depression medication. I also knew that he was capable of physical violence and that he had been in trouble with our local policemen on other occasions. My phone calls to his home and attempts to contact his mother were unsuccessful. Later that night, Todd emailed me:

> Dear Mrs. Heird,
> When you talked to me after school today I was very Below the Line and Top 20 saved my future. I was about to assault someone who I had a rivalry with. Instead I Top 20'd it and instead of going to jail I talked to another Top 20 student, trampolined and went home happy.
> Thanks for so much,
> Todd

"Todd is now a successful freshman in our high school, controlling his bi-polar condition and working a part-time job. His parents are extremely happy for what has taken place in their son. Thank you for the positive impact Top 20 is making in our young people."

Todd was fortunate to have met a Top 20 teacher who still wanted to learn and grow at the end of her career. Although Pat retired from counseling and teaching in June of 2008, she's not done yet. Since then she has coordinated Top 20 training sessions for every teacher in the Windsor School District. Pat's kaizen is impacting parents, educators and community leaders not only in her home community, but also throughout northern Colorado and Utah.

Top 20 teachers have the power to make a positive difference and kaizen keeps that power alive for many years.

## ROOKIES' KAIZEN

Kaizen is a philosophy not only to be practiced by wise veteran teachers to give purpose to their last years in schools, but also to be implemented early in a new teacher's career. Recent college graduates, who often receive many Not Good Enough messages in their first years in the classroom, develop negative mental habits and behaviors to compensate. New teachers frequently confess, "I felt so insecure and incompetent that I didn't know how to properly maintain classroom order. I'd scream at my students like a dictator. It worked to keep them quiet, but I didn't have great relationships with kids."

New teachers may also feel intimidated by the overwhelming amount of preparation and content that goes into teaching.

**TRUE TALES**

Although never having taken a class on Latin America herself, Willow was hired to teach Latin American geography to freshmen. One day a student asked, "Miss Sweeney, what is the major agricultural crop of Peru?" Willow confidently replied, "Corn." Having no idea what the main crop of Peru was, Willow lied. The student's question had activated a feeling of Not Good Enough inside the new teacher.

Once the students found out that corn was not the right answer, they lacked trust in their teacher. Willow quickly realized that where there is a lack of trust, there is a lack of learning. She vowed to be honest to her students. When she didn't know the answer to a question, her new response became, "You know, I don't know the answer to that question. Let's look it up together." Students respected that answer and Willow no longer felt Not Good Enough when she didn't know everything about everything.

Maureen Mohan is a budding Top 20 teacher passionate about kaizen. She attended a Top 20 Training session a month before she began her first year of teaching in the fall of 2008. Not only are her students in a Chicago high school learning English literature and how to write, but also Maureen is learning about her students, her profession and herself.

Maureen's kaizen has taken the form of personal reflection, which she titled, *Important Things I Learned My First Year of Teaching*. Some of her insights include:

- Set the tone for the year on the first day and sustain it.
- A soft voice rather than a loud one gains students' attention.
- Students won't remember all you taught them, but they will remember how you treated them.
- Respect your students and celebrate all their successes.
- Listen carefully to parents before you respond.
- All students can learn.
- Thank students who correct your typos and spelling errors.
- Remain calm in a difficult conversation and your words will have more impact.
- Don't expect perfection, but be willing to work towards it.
- Be willing to give students responsibility and choice.

Kaizen has led this young woman through the confusion of being a first year teacher. It has provided her with a clearer focus on what is important and a stronger belief in herself. Instead of hiding her confusion and limitations as a first year teacher, Maureen has grown and learned from her experience. She is now better able to lead her students through the confusion and self-doubt that is inevitable in school and during adolescence. Like Gandhi, she can now speak with a voice that can be understood by her students.

## OUR NEED FOR HUMILITY

As teachers, we are experts. We have skills and knowledge, especially about our particular subject area. We are expected to know the answers. When we don't know the answer, our Not Good Enough button can get activated and manifest itself in our resistance to growth or learning.

**Our desire for kaizen is rooted in humility.** It is based in the awareness that we don't know everything. It is based in the awareness that there are teaching practices and skills that we have not sufficiently developed. Lacking knowledge or certain skills does not mean we can't be effective teachers. Lack of kaizen does.

Top 20 teachers desire growth and learning more than approval or the appearance of knowing it all. Their humility and curiosity bring them to a place where they and their students need to be...kaizen.

# TIME FOR REFLECTION & ACTION

1. How strong is your desire for kaizen?

2. Identify an area in your professional life where you want to improve? Give some thought to how you might make this happen.

3. Is there an area of growth or learning to which you are experiencing some resistance?

4. What did you become aware of while reading this chapter regarding an action you would like to take? What action would you like to take?

# Part 2:
# Coaching America's Youth

Coaches, moderators, advisors and activity directors play a major role in determining a student's school experience. Just like teachers in the classroom, a revolution is also necessary for those of us who coach athletic teams or direct other co-curricular activities.

In many situations, coaches and moderators have a bigger impact on students than classroom teachers. One reason for this is that the athletic field or the theatrical stage is a more public arena for young people. Although a student's performance in a classroom or science lab is personal, it is much more private. However, what a student does during a basketball game or a debate meet is viewed by many.

Furthermore, young people do not usually *choose* to attend history or health class the same way they *choose* to attend pep band, gymnastics or soccer. Students attending co-curricular activities are generally coming with a greater interest, willingness and motivation. This offers an even greater opportunity to affect their lives.

The next four chapters (15-18) of the book provide thoughts about how we might consider this special role and opportunity.

To make these chapters more readable, the word *coach* will be used to cover a broad list of areas: athletic coaches, band and drama directors, moderators, advisors and coordinators of special activities such as student council, yearbook and chess clubs.

The definition of *coach,* as in stagecoach, is to bring someone to a different place. We are using the word *coach* to mean someone who helps others get to where they want to go.

# Top 20 Coaches

Top 20 coaches are teachers, too. This chapter looks back at the first part of this book and applies teahing concepts from those chapters to our various coaching situations. Chapter 15 reviews the previous fourteen chapters for thoughts or tools to foster Top 20 experiences and develop the potential of individual participants or teams.

## Chapter 1
## Have Power to Make a Positive Difference

**SUCCESS = GOOD RESULTS + GOOD RIDE** The tendency in co-curricular activities is to focus solely on the first part of this equation, the Results. We tend to look closely at the finished product, whether it is the quality of the yearbook published or the won–lost record of the softball team. Top 20 coaches are ever-aware of the *Ride* as well, keeping a watchful eye on how the yearbook staff operates as a team and how the girls on the softball bench conduct themselves when they are not participating.

**SUCCESS = P1 x P2 x P3** In Chapter 1, the formula for success was: S = IQ x EQ. For students involved in sports and other co-curricular activities, we are going to redefine that formula: Success = P1 x P2 x P3.

**P1 = Inside Power    P2 = Physical Power or Talent    P3 = Outside Power**

P1 or Inside Power is a student's awareness of her thoughts or beliefs. P2 or Physical Power and Talent is a student's skill or ability level. For kids in sports, it includes their athletic ability. For kids in band, it's their musical ability. For kids working on the school newspaper, it's their writing ability. P3 or Outside Power is what a student communicates to others, the positive or negative energy he projects.

As coaches, we spend most of our time with students trying to develop P2. As important as that is, the overall experience that students have in co-curricular activities may have more to do with P1 and P3.

Throughout this entire book we are really focusing on P1 and P3. These are the vital Thinking, Learning and Communicating skills that can be developed in every co-curricular activity. They go a long way in determining whether a team or organization will wind up with a Top 20 or Bottom 80 experience. They also go a long way in developing the skills that will help students be successful in life after school and sports. Essential to the revolution in coaching is that we give these areas ample time as we work with young people.

**BEWARE OF THE LIE** Top 20 coaches know that success in athletics or other co-curricular activities is by no means a guarantee of success in future life. It's important to point this out to young people as they participate in school activities. Top 20 coaches do this time and time again because outside sources (like parents, the media or Bottom 80 coaches) are sometimes delivering a far different message.

# Chapter 2
# Know How to See Things Differently

**BASIC CHANGE MODEL** What keeps coaches awake in the middle of the night is usually related to something we are not getting from our team or organization. Typical Bottom 80 responses are to change nothing, change what we do or blame. These three dysfunctional responses are almost always connected to our need to be right.

Looking back at his high school softball coaching days, Tom was guilty of all three at times. When his team was not winning, Tom would make no changes in his practice plans or the line-up, but would routinely put the blame on the pitcher or the umpire instead. Though Tom was unaware at that time, this kept him and his team *stuck in yuck*. He didn't realize that curiosity and the SEE corner of the Frame were where the solution could be found.

## THREE RIGHTS: R = R+

At times, coaches might be right, but there is always more to the story.

> In his first year as a high school girls' basketball coach, Tom held an early morning Saturday practice for his team. Since Barb was not there on time, Tom made the rest of the team run laps until Barb arrived. His intent was to punish the whole team in hopes that Barb would feel bad and the other girls would learn from making her an example. When Barb did appear fifteen minutes late, the other players began giggling. Tom assigned the girls more running to punish this obvious show of disrespect. It was only after practice that Barb showed Tom why she had arrived late. She had been waiting for the bakery to finish icing *his* birthday cake.

Tom had been right about Barb being tardy. However, his judgment and lack of curiosity created an embarrassing experience for him and a disappointing experience for his team.

## PARADIGM SHIFTS: SEEING THINGS DIFFERENTLY

The ability to ask others how they see it is a valuable tool in every coach's toolbox. Unfortunately this tool is usually in mint condition, since it is so rarely used. Top 20 coaches ask for help. They know that no two people see anything exactly the same way. A highly successful coach once asked Tom to scout his boys' team, even though Tom was coaching girls at the time. This coach was interested in hearing a completely objective outside opinion about how he was handling his team. His openness, humility and willingness allowed him to see more and make a positive difference in his season.

# Chapter 3
# Are Aware of Their Thinking
# and Live Above the Line

## LIFE LOOKS DIFFERENT

Top 20s are aware of their thinking, especially in the heat of battle. They are wary of their thinking and decision-making when they go Below the Line. This is particularly important when interactions occur with game officials and players' parents.

Willow was often frustrated with her golf team's practices. She'd rush out of school to get to the course. She was determined to start drills immediately and would be upset when the team wanted to visit and goof around. She'd think, "They're not taking this seriously. I've been working all day and now I'm stuck listening to 15-year-old girls talk about their lives." As her annoyance grew, she'd say, "Girls, this isn't social hour. No more talking." Her reaction invited everyone to go Below the Line.

Being tired from teaching all day, Willow realized she was Below the Line and seeing her team in a negative way. This awareness allowed her to feel empathy for the girls who also were tired from a day in school. Visiting with each other was their way of rising Above the Line. Willow then decided to hold practices 45 minutes after school. It gave her and the team a chance to relax and refocus. Once the team arrived, Willow would ask them to take five minutes to talk to each other and chat with her. This allowed everyone to move Above the Line and have a positive and productive practice.

## DECISIONS BECOME MESSES  Coaches get many Invitations to go Below the Line.

Tom was coaching in a City Championship basketball game that had degenerated into a wild, foul-filled, hostile contest. The crowd had joined the fray as well, with the situation escalating into a frenzied atmosphere late in the game. Unaware that he had fallen well Below the Line, Tom stood up and screamed, "Time out!" The referees asked Tom whether he was requesting a thirty-second or a sixty-second time out. "That's up to you two," Tom sarcastically yelled so the crowd could hear. "I took the time out so that you two could take a breather and figure out what's going on out here!"

The officials were not pleased with Tom's *helpful suggestion*. Besides giving him a technical foul, they filed a complaint with the state league office. After a couple administrative meetings, Tom cleaned up some of the mess he had made. However, years later, some people still base their opinion of Tom on that Below the Line decision.

# Chapter 4
# Create Connections

**COMMUNICATING "YOU MATTER"** A student's name, voice and sense of belonging are vital in the classroom, but they are equally important in any co-curricular activity. Top 20 leaders have to be extra careful about how they treat each individual they coach.

Some players will get preferential treatment when it comes to playing time, post-season awards or media attention. That's unavoidable. While some members of the concert band might earn first chair or all-state status, every band member's name and voice must be honored to ensure that she has an equal feeling of worth and belonging. While one trumpet player might sit first chair at the concert, the band director should make sure that everyone gets a turn to sit *first chair* on the bus ride home.

# Chapter 5
# Know the Power of Messages and Beliefs

**MESSAGES FROM THE CIRCUMFERENCE** Many coaches are unaware of the impact of their messages on young people. What we **intend** to communicate may be very different from the **impact** of our message. A seemingly harmless remark by a trusted mentor can be very harmful to a youngster.

After a rainy and cold golf meet, Willow's team came into the clubhouse and circled around the table where she was sitting. Willow sensed immediately that things had not gone well for her players. They looked exhausted and sad. After sharing their scores, the captain asked, "Coach, are you mad we played so bad?" Willow, shocked that her players thought she would be angry, said, "Of course I'm not mad. I guess I'm just disappointed." At this some of the girls started crying. One player said, "We would much rather have you be mad, than disappointed."

Although not Willow's intent, telling the girls that they disappointed her made them feel like failures.

Many of these messages can be non-verbal in nature. If a drama director rolls her eyes at a high school actor during a rehearsal, that message immediately become a Not Good Enough belief. Coaches' sideline gestures and facial expressions can be equally damaging.

Sometimes a coach responds to a player's mistake with a negative non-verbal (throwing his hands into the air in disgust) that is actually intended to send this message to the crowd: "She really messed that play up, didn't she? I certainly covered this in practice so it's obviously not my fault, folks."

**THE BAMBOO TREE: PERSISTENCE** Top 20 coaches know that they need to send *You're good enough* messages to their young people time and time again. Because so many negative messages exist in a youngster's world, coaches need to persistently combat those with encouraging words.

The bamboo tree reminds us that we might not reap the fruit of these efforts in the short term. A tennis coach might easily become frustrated when her efforts to change a young player's bad habits do not seem to be making a difference. "I've tried to get her to stop cursing on the court for two years," the coach might complain, "and she's still doing it." Top 20s know that persistence will pay off, that continued belief in that young player will eventually produce positive results, even if it happens three years later on the college tennis team.

# Chapter 6
# Create Safety
# and a Positive Work Environment

**HELP OTHERS SUCCEED** This life skill is probably even more teachable outside the classroom than inside. One of the most important life lessons that we can teach youngsters is how to help teammates succeed. Many times after a game, coaches or team members will point out positive things about the game or outstanding individual achievements. But Top 20 coaches go a step further. After a game or during practice the next day, they ask, "Can anyone give me an example of how one of us helped another teammate succeed in the game?" Pointing out a player's unselfish pass or an encouraging word from a bench player can go a long way in promoting this value.

## HONOR THE ABSENT

Safety is imperative for any group or team to thrive. Nothing is more harmful to the emotional safety of a group than the dishonoring of its absent members.

Dishonoring Example: "Tim's gone again...third time this month. Obviously he doesn't care about this team."

Honoring Example: "Tim's gone again...third time this month. I'll give him a call and see if he's okay."

While it is important for a baseball team to practice bunting, it might be even more important to spend some practice time on Honoring the Absent. This could be as simple as taking time to ask the team, "How have we been doing this week at Honoring the Absent?" Coaches could ask the players to rate this on a scale of one (terrible) to ten (outstanding) with a hands-up vote. If the results are not what a team would hope for, they could establish a few guidelines, work on them and assess the improvement a week later.

# Chapter 7
# Listen to Understand

Coaches have a unique advantage over teachers when it comes to teaching young people about listening and focus levels. Students might not *want* to be in math class, but they probably attend basketball practice by choice. While a B+ grade might be a desired outcome of listening better in science, a starting position at shortstop might be an even more effective carrot to dangle.

Athletes, actors, musicians or any young person attempting to reach his potential as a performer will most certainly benefit from operating in the Zone. Once a young person has discovered the pitfalls of Life on My Mind,

Judgmental, Distracted and Processing, this awareness can make a huge impact on his concentration, focus and ultimately his performance.

Coaches get plenty of rainouts, late buses and awkward gym times. These times can easily be used to teach concepts like this one. Spending an hour or two during the season teaching **Not Now** and **Parking Lot** could make a dynamic difference in the development of young people and their teams.

# Chapter 8
# Help Students Move Outside
# Their Comfort Zone

## FEAR OF FAILURE

**FEAR OF FAILURE**  We will only get maximum performance from students participating in sports or other activities if youngsters are not paralyzed by this fear. The sign, **Failure Is An Event, Not A Person,** could make a huge difference in the development of a player or a team.

Students also have to learn how to deal with Other People's Opinions. Unfortunately, many youngsters fear OPOs more than they fear for their own safety. They constantly analyze how their successes and failures on the field and off impact other's assessment of them as people. As their coaches, we can help them discount opinions of others that are not in their best interest.

Any person's Core self (her worth, identity and purpose) should be unaffected by a dropped pass, a strikeout or a poor speech performance. Top 20 coaches remind their young learners of this at every opportunity. They should also be quick to remind their athletes that their successes are also nothing more than events, and that they have no impact whatsoever on their Core. Learning these lessons early in life will benefit students well beyond their school years.

## OUR RESPONSES TO MISTAKES

**OUR RESPONSES TO MISTAKES**  Coaches should be alert for the Bottom 80 responses to mistakes that will inevitably pop up in their participants. Young people will deny, hide and justify their mistakes; they will assign blame and dwell on their errors.

When these behaviors occur, the time is ripe for mentoring young people around owning their mistakes and learning the lessons hidden therein. The absolute best way to teach this is to model it.

Tom's girls' basketball team once lost a big conference game to a team with less individual talent. The opponents sprung a surprise zone press on Tom's team, a defensive move that lead to the upset win. After the game, Tom's players fully expected their coach to place the blame squarely on their shoulders, as he had in previous situations. Instead, Tom had a moment of Top 20 clarity en route to the locker room. He owned the mistake himself, told the players that he had not prepared them properly and promised that the team would never fall victim to that defensive ploy again.

From that point on in the season, there was a massive, tangible shift in the culture of the team. Players became more willing to own their own mistakes once they observed that the leader was willing to do the same. Learning those lessons led that 13-16 (won-loss) team to the state tournament that year.

## NO NEUTRAL RESPONSE TO A MISTAKE   Youngsters involved in co-curricular activities constantly fail or make mistakes. They miss shots in basketball, commit errors in baseball and stumble delivering their lines in the school play. A coach's response in these situations is powerful, especially because these are public events. A harsh response will perpetuate a youngster's fear of failure and keep her locked inside her Comfort Zone. A pat on the back or supportive comment will help her deal with mistakes more productively.

# Chapter 9
# Keep Stupid in the Box

## LETTING STUPID OUT OF THE BOX   The stakes are higher for co-curricular participants that perform publicly. It is one thing to feel stupid when students are all alone at home trying to figure out

Shakespeare, but it is far more likely that that feeling will arise when they:

- Drop the touchdown pass at the Homecoming game.
- Freeze up on the stage and forget their lines.
- Get picked off third base with the score tied.
- Trip and fall during a dance competition.

Coaches have to keep a watchful eye on the equal sign (=) during these vulnerable times in a young person's life. We are not proposing that youngsters avoid situations where they might fail or become embarrassed. Nor should we overpraise where not appropriate. We are suggesting that adults mentor students to be aware and not correlate a loss or a mistake with being stupid.

## CAUSES OF STUPID: CONFUSION

This cause of stupid is even more dangerous for participants in co-curricular activities, especially when experienced in front of their peers, families or other spectators.

If an athlete advances from youth sports to the 9th grade team to the junior varsity to the varsity, confusion will be a natural part of that progression. Even the most outstanding athletes will eventually run into that level where they cannot always excel. NBA superstar LeBron James experienced confusion during his first year (2003-04) in professional basketball. James had his lowest scoring average and shooting percentage as he transitioned from high school basketball to the pro ranks. If James had put up the equal sign during that season and deemed himself stupid or Not Good Enough, it is doubtful that he would have developed so quickly into a top NBA player.

We cannot remove confusion from the co-curricular experience. Participating in debate, tennis or mock trial will most certainly challenge young people and provide confusing situations for them. What we can do is change confusion's bad reputation. We can celebrate confusion as an integral part of the learning process. We can remind students that confusion is what happens right before they have a realization that makes a big difference in their performance. We have to encourage them through the confusion by saying things like, "It's okay. You just don't get it *yet*. The only way to get it is to keep going."

# Chapter 10
# Answer the Relevancy Question: What's in It for Me?

## LEARNING 'IN THE MOMENT' AND 'AFTER THE FACT'

Top 20 coaches are aware that young people learn, make connections and get insights in different ways. Some athletes or participants need just one or two repetitions to learn how to use new information, move across the stage or run an out-of-bounds play. Others might require numerous repetitions to get the realization.

Coaches frequently become frustrated when they present a new play or new information to their team and some of the players struggle to understand the concept immediately. This can be an invitation to go Below the Line. Often the players will react to their own confusion by pretending:

> "Does everyone know what they're doing now?" the coach will ask his team. "What about you, Sam?" Sam will almost always smile and nod his head, knowing full-well that he has no idea what the coach is talking about.

The Top 20 approach to this problem is to let the young people know that confusion is part of the process in this activity and that some people will get realizations After the Fact.

## WHAT'S IN IT FOR ME? STAR QUALITIES!

Star Qualities are those powerful intangibles that help us deal effectively with life's challenges.

> Tom's 1995 girls' basketball team (the 13-16 team that made it to the state tournament) is a shining example of "What's in it for me?" in sports or co-curriculars. This group was not the fastest, tallest or most athletically talented team. What made the team special was the players' individual Star Qualities, those *soft* skills like persistence, teamwork, optimism and self-motivation. Because these qualities characterized the team as a whole, there were many times that the team found ways to upset more physically talented teams.

The players from that team are now in their early thirties, using those same Star Qualities to make a positive difference in their own and others' lives. They are successful physical therapists, dentists, nurses, athletic directors and attorneys. They are also successful wives, mothers, board members and citizens. Very few of them have touched a basketball in the past decade, but they have used the Star Qualities they learned in that sport every day.

# Chapter 11
# Stop the Spread of Negativity
# in Themselves and Their School

**TORNADOES** Coaches who do not acknowledge the existence of group negativity and deal with it in some meaningful manner will not bring out the best in their teams. Potential can only develop when a group feels safe. Tornadoes undermine safety.

Top 20 leaders know when a tornado watch is in effect. They know that there are times when team negativity is likely to arise. Tornadoes might develop:

- After a tough loss, especially if controversial officials' calls were involved.
- After a game where many players did not have the opportunity to participate.
- After one player is acknowledged with media attention or an all-conference award.
- During a pre-season or post-season meeting with parents.

It is vital to take the necessary time to deal with these situations head-on. Ignoring real tornadoes in Kansas is not an effective way to deal with the physical dangers they carry. Ignoring social tornadoes is just as dangerous.

**THOUGHT CIRCLES** The same is true of individual negativity. Coaches should provide young players with the tools to deal with the mental challenges, not just the physical ones, that co-curriculars bring. Thought Circles will be a natural part of leaving the Comfort Zone in sports or activities. Youngsters will routinely take a small piece of factual information (a substitute replacing them during a game or meet) and mentally evolve it into an enormous problem (deciding that the coach hates them). Coaches and their assistants need to make sure during competitions and practices that their players are monitoring their thinking skills as well as their physical skills.

# Chapter 12
# Resolve Conflicts Effectively

**DEALING WITH PLAYERS** For coaches to deal with conflict effectively, it is essential that we are aware of being Above or Below the Line. When a coach or player has gone Below the Line, there is little hope for any conflict to be resolved. Resolution requires our best thinking, not our worst. Resolving conflicts in the heat of practice or competition is pretty much an oxymoron. Therefore, we will often be more effective if we deal with the conflict *later* when we are Above the Line rather than *now* when we are Below the Line.

> Towards the end of his coaching career, Tom made a point of changing his post-game routine. His old script generally included negative locker room tirades that produced unresolvable conflicts. Realizing the ineffectiveness of this behavior, he had his players share only positive comments about the team or its players after every game. If there were issues to be dealt with, the next day's practice would be the place to do that.

**T**RUE **T**ALES

**DEALING WITH PARENTS** Coaches often point to conflicts with parents as one of the main obstacles to successful seasons. They routinely encounter parents who have inflated opinions about their youngsters' abilities and who question policies and decisions. In many cases, the ensuing conflicts create those gnawing feelings of regret, confusion and anger that keep coaches awake late at night.

A major factor to consider in this complicated equation is the Frame. The Seeing, Feeling and Doing of the coach is frequently in direct opposition to that of the parents:

|  | **Coach** | **Parent** |
|---|---|---|
| **SEE** | Athlete is a player on the team (team comes first, individual second) | Athlete is beloved son or daughter (child comes first, team second) |
| **FEEL** | Defensive & threatened | Defensive & threatened |
| **DO** | Act in team's best interest | Act in child's best interest |
| **GET** | Conflict & phone calls | Conflict & frustration |

Top 20 coaches are fully aware of this difference in the Frames. They take steps to make this clear to all parties, emphasizing that it is natural and expected. Paul made this discussion a key element of his pre-season meeting with parents every year. He found that it was a positive step towards more effective communication with parents.

## DEALING WITH OFFICIALS
Interactions with game officials, referees, judges and umpires are another chief source of irritation for coaches. Many times during contests, a coach's frustration with her team's play or with her own performance results in a conflict with an official.

Doing it later is not an option here. Re-framing the situation can be helpful, but sometimes difficult to pull off in the heat of the moment. Remembering that there will be a *next time* is crucial. Unless a coach plans to retire at the end of the game she is coaching that night, there will likely be a *next time* encounter with that same official.

Not every conflict with an official will result in the decision that pleases the Top 20 coach. It cannot be a Win-Win situation when it comes to which team will get possession of the basketball after a given play. One team will get the ball; the other will not. However, it can always be Win-Win when it is about the level of professionalism and dignified behavior between the adults involved (coach and referee). Their behavior during a conflict is a model for the fans and the young people they are supervising. When coaches monitor themselves and behave in a way that expresses positive values, they set up successful future *next time* experiences with officials.

# Chapter 13
# Are Aware of What Gets Activated in Them

## ACTIVATING 'NOT GOOD ENOUGH'
Just as teachers face their own *hit* lists, coaches also face daily challenges that invite them to head Below the Line. Unlike those that happen in the classroom, many of these random negative events occur in public settings. Some of the most common coaching *hits* might happen when:

- Controversial calls are made by game officials.
- Players make mistakes.
- Players miss practices.
- Practice plans are changed due to facility conflicts.
- Parents question coaching decisions.
- Athletic directors give critical feedback.
- Other coaches succeed or receive awards.

Coaches' indicators can be even more dangerous than teachers' indicators, especially when they come out in public arenas. Some of the most common dysfunctional coaching behaviors might include:

- Making sarcastic negative comments to players.
- Yelling at and belittling players.
- Making empty threats.
- Demonstrating negative non-verbals at games.
- Throwing tantrums in confrontations with officials.
- Treating opposing players and coaches in an unprofessional manner.

## BECOMING AWARE OF OUR POWER TO MAKE CHOICES
Most of us entered the coaching profession because of strong beliefs and positive values regarding the formation of young people. These values generally revolve around maintaining personal dignity, providing a positive role model and treating children with respect. Much like teachers, coaches tend to display those values most of the time when they are dealing with young people. During times of Below the Line challenges, however, these values can easily be neglected.

Remember, when *hits* occur and we are unaware of our own emotional instability, the reactions come instantaneously and are usually not based on personal values. When we can monitor these negative situations, stay Above the Line and insert even the most minimal pause, we can drastically change the outcome of the event. If we pause between the *hit* and the reaction, we are more likely to insert what we truly value into the situation and get better results.

# Chapter 14
# Top 20 Teachers Practice Kaizen

**ROOKIES' AND VETERANS' KAIZEN** Top 20 coaches young and old need to seek continual improvement, both personally and professionally. It is common for veteran coaches to become complacent and get stuck in a rut with their choices, opinions and behaviors. Even though they may have established themselves in their profession, the most successful veteran coaches seek input from others. This input can come from players, administrators, parents or their fellow coaches. **Kaizen is what distinguishes great coaches from good coaches.**

Young coaches have a special need for input and guidance. Often, promising coaches' careers are cut short by misguided, inexperienced decisions that result in disastrous outcomes. Their poor choices are fueled by the feeling of "I'm Not Good Enough" when they get negative messages from various sources early in their careers. Incremental, gradual improvement and growth (kaizen) does not happen just because coaches get older. Rather, it happens intentionally when young coaches are mentored, nurtured and guided in a manner that makes a positive difference.

**OUR NEED FOR HUMILITY** Just like their counterparts in the classroom, coaches are fully aware that humility is the first step toward kaizen. Only those coaches that value curiosity more than they value approval from others will seek this type of personal and professional growth. What usually stands in the way of humility is our need to be right or to appear to be in control at all times. Top 20 coaches know that this need to be right has to be put aside if they are to fully experience kaizen.

# CHAPTER 16

## Top 20 Coaches
# Provide Many Answers to the Question: How'd Ya Do?

Mr. O'Malley, a custodian at Waldorf High School, was working in the cafeteria when the varsity and junior varsity girls' basketball teams returned from their games.

"Jordan," he said to the captain of the varsity team, "how'd ya do?"

"We won," said Jordan smiling. "Thanks for asking, Mr. O'Malley."

As the last girl entered the building, Mr. O'Malley asked, "Brittany, how'd ya do?"

The sad faced member of the junior varsity team responded, "We lost, Mr. O'Malley."

Jordan's and Brittany's answers to Mr. O'Malley's question are quite common. Following a competitive activity, almost every student who is asked "How'd ya do?" will answer by saying, "We won" or "We lost."

Co-curricular activities play an enormous role in students' lives. Students spend countless hours after school practicing and rehearsing to develop their talents in order to succeed in sports and other events. They fill their summers practicing on their own or attending team practices or camps in order to further develop their skills. Parents support their sons and daughters by attending games, driving them to events and paying hundreds and sometimes thousands of dollars for equipment, activities fees and camp registration costs.

The amount of time, energy and money that goes into creating these opportunities for students on the part of parents, coaches, the school district, taxpayers and youth themselves is enormous. If the only things young people are getting out of these experiences are letter jackets, trophies and a record of wins and losses, then it is hardly worth the effort that so many make.

**RUE ALES**

Tom coached high school girls' basketball for 21 years. Many of his teams won conference and section championships. A few of his teams that had brilliant won-loss records turned out to be the least successful groups he coached. Altough they produced victories, they did not experience teamwork, life lessons or lasting relationships. One year, Tom's 13-16 (won-loss record) team shockingly made it all the way to the state tournament. This team played together, learned together and matured together. Many of the players on that team are still close friends. It's actually the most successful group Tom ever coached.

Top 20 coaches value co-curricular opportunities for students because of a wide range of benefits participation in these activities offers young people. Consequently, they help students participating in co-curriculars to consider a number of other responses to the question *How'd ya do?* As they work with students, Top 20 coaches help them realize the importance of each of these areas.

## 1. HOW'D YA DO: DID YOU WIN OR LOSE?

Winning and losing are significant events in kids' lives. Top 20 coaches realize that both winning and losing offer wonderful and potentially dangerous results for young people. Students who experience winning benefit by learning that they have what it takes to be successful. This can help develop their confidence and motivate them to strive for even greater challenges.

On the other hand, winning has such a high value in our culture that it can create pressure on youth to win at all costs. Contemporary concerns stemming from this way of thinking are the cheating and the increased use of steroids and other performance-enhancing products by young athletes. Furthermore, the emphasis on winning can result in young people believing that their inner worth only comes from achievement.

If guided properly, kids can benefit from losing. Learning how to deal with losses in an athletic event can help students deal with losses they will inevitably experience later in life. Losing provides a healthy perspective. It keeps us humble and highlights areas where improvement can be made. Although it can happen by winning as well, losing also provides opportunities that strengthen the bonds between kids.

Constantly losing without having significant experiences of success can diminish a student's confidence. It can develop in a youngster a reluctance to try things in the future unless success is assured. The fear of failing or losing can keep kids in their Comfort Zone. A *loser's* mentality can influence a student to withdraw from life and not engage in healthy risk taking activities.

Top 20 coaches know that young people have three options: winning, losing and not participating. The first two options are greatly preferred over sitting out. The reason for this is because kids can experience so many other wonderful things when they are involved in band, drama, clubs, sports or other co-curricular activities. Showing up and either winning or losing is much more beneficial for our young people than not showing up at all.

**Hey, how'd ya do? Did you win or lose?**

## 2. HOW'D YA DO: DID YOU HAVE FUN?

If we watched young children at play, what would be the most notable thing we would observe about them? They are having fun. Having fun by playing is truly recreation. Whether it is the stress that young people experience in school or work or in their relationships with other people, having fun allows an outlet in which they can be re-created. Play and fun refresh the human spirit.

For many adults, however, recreation is more like *wreck*-reation. We are driven as we play games to compete with a necessity to win and prove our worth. What is it that makes a grown person swear and throw a golf club when that little white ball doesn't go straight? Our play is often not about having fun but getting stressed out.

Of the nine things being presented in this chapter on *How'd ya do*, the one that is most important to young people is having fun. Top 20 coaches accept their responsibility to direct practices and co-curricular activities in such a manner that young people have fun.

This doesn't mean, of course, that it's only fun. Hard work, adversity, disappointment and not getting everything a kid wants should also be part of the experience. Top 20 coaches balance these with enjoyment.

**Hey, how'd ya do? Did you have fun?**

## 3. HOW'D YA DO: DID YOU LEARN ANYTHING?

Co-curricular activities offer numerous opportunities to learn about all sorts of things. Students can learn more about the particular game or activity in which they are participating. They can learn about themselves and others. Athletes can learn how to strengthen and care for their own bodies and how to mentally prepare themselves for competition.

Top 20 coaches realize that sports and other co-curriculars are part of the overall educational experience of students. After-school activities like student council, lacrosse or mock trial are simply extensions of the school day. As such, Top 20 coaches help young people discover the powerful life lessons that are available in these activities. Some of these lessons will help students work more effectively with others throughout their lives.

Besides focusing on touchdowns, rebounds and musical instruments, Top 20 coaches open youngsters up to these possibilities by sharing things they themselves are learning and asking students what they are getting from these experiences.

**Hey, how'd ya do? Did you learn anything?**

## 4. HOW'D YA DO: DID YOU IMPROVE SINCE LAST TIME?

The road to doing our best is made up of frequent moments of continual improvement. Whether it is a particular skill, understanding the game or working together as a team, Top 20 coaches help students improve from week to week.

We can encourage continual improvement in our young people by helping them develop realistic goals. Having goals and strategies for meeting those goals provide students with a road map for progress. As they work towards accomplishing these goals, they discover their own internal power for enhancing their lives.

We cannot improve by only doing what we can already do. By expecting improvement, Top 20 coaches encourage students to stretch outside their Comfort Zone. This expectation helps students overcome the fear of failure and the fear of making mistakes.

**Hey, how'd ya do? Did you improve since last time?**

## 5. HOW'D YA DO: DID YOU HELP SOMEONE ELSE SUCCEED?

One of the most important things a young person can learn if she is to succeed in life is how to help other people succeed. Jennie Docherty is a gifted long distance runner. She received All-State honors in track and field in high school. Jennie also played basketball for four years in high school. Not as gifted as a basketball player, Jennie saw very little playing time during her senior year, getting into only a half dozen games all season.

Nonetheless, teammates considered Jennie one of the most valuable players on the team. Every day in practice she helped her teammates to get better. She modeled hard work and dedication by pushing herself in every drill even though it never resulted in more playing time. She was a constant support to the younger girls on the team by encouraging them when they made a mistake and helping them learn what they were supposed to do. During games she would spot a weakness in the opponent's defense and recommend to her coach a play that would give her team an edge. Almost everything Jennie did throughout her senior year made her team and her teammates better.

Jennie did this on her own. It was not expected of her. But it ought to have been. **It ought to be an expectation of every student that she helps others succeed.** Top 20 coaches convey that expectation to their students. They help them become aware of the importance of this and provide opportunities for it to happen. By helping young people help others succeed, Top 20 coaches guide these students down the most direct route to their own success.

**Hey, how'd ya do? Did you help someone else succeed?**

# 6. HOW'D YA DO: DID YOU CONDUCT YOURSELF WELL?

Many times in the heat of an athletic contest, players, coaches and fans lose sight of their values and act in ways that tarnish their reputation. Embarrassing behavior on the court, on the sidelines and in the stands has unfortunately become the norm in many athletic events. As a rule, players, coaches and spectators regret those negative behaviors almost immediately after the contest.

Top 20 coaches are vigilant about their teams' and fans' behavior during events. No matter how the ball bounces or how the umpire's calls go, Top 20 coaches always do their best to maintain dignity, composure and perspective. Remember, eventually we have to ask ourselves:

**Hey, how'd ya do? Did you conduct yourself well?**

## 7. HOW'D YA DO: DID YOU DO YOUR BEST?

John Wooden, the legendary basketball coach of the UCLA Bruins, used the question "Did you do your best?" to define success.

> "Success is peace of mind, which is a direct result of self-satisfaction in knowing you did your best to become the best you are capable of becoming."

Wooden did not coach his players to be better than someone else. He did not coach his team to compare themselves to others. He did not coach his team to win. He coached his team to be the best that they could be as a team. The fact that UCLA won 88 consecutive basketball games and twelve national championships resulted from their achieving that more fundamental success of being **"the best you are capable of becoming."**

**TRUE TALES**

Paul had an inspirational football coach. Jim Troglio's way of instilling Coach Wooden's philosophy in high school boys was the Mirror Test. After every game he would ask his players to walk in front of the mirror in the locker room. Still wearing their football helmets and uniforms, each player would look in the mirror and silently ask himself, "Did I do my best?"

Coach Troglio had mentored his players to realize that the answer to this question had nothing to do with the score and it had nothing to do with winning or losing the game. It had nothing to do with outside conditions or circumstances. Rather, it had everything to do with what was going on inside each player. Had he focused during practice and the game or had he been distracted? Had he been unselfish or selfish? Had he taken responsibility for his role or did he blame others? Had he given it his all during conditioning drills or did he try to cut corners? Did he do his best?

The team had an undefeated season until losing by one point in the last game. The headlines in the sports section of the newspaper the next day read, "Bruins Spoil Undefeated Season."

But what really happened during that season? Did this football team do its best? As the players drove home together after each game or hung out at the local hamburger joint, they would often ask each other how they responded to the Mirror Test. After all of their victories, even though they had won by three, four or more touchdowns, no one on the team

144

felt that he had done his best. However, as every kid paraded before the mirror after the team's lone loss, every player responded inside by saying, "Yes, I did my best."

Was it a spoiled undefeated season? Not to the 35 athletes who experienced the satisfaction for the first time of having done their best.

Top 20 coaches like John Wooden and Jim Troglio remind their players of the deeper and more meaningful experience that is available to them by striving to do their best.

**Hey, how'd ya do? Did you do your best?**

# 8. HOW'D YA DO: DID YOU APPRECIATE ANYTHING ABOUT YOUR OPPONENTS?

Opponent does not mean enemy. Yet if aliens from outer space observed many of our athletic events, it is not likely that they would notice a difference between those two words. Often fans, athletes and coaches treat opponents as if they are the enemy.

Paul had stolen 32 consecutive bases while playing baseball during his senior year in high school. Jim Mohan, the second baseman from Streator High School, was the only player to ever tag him out trying to steal a base.

Even though an opponent, there was much to admire and appreciate about Jim. He played as if he really enjoyed the game and his teammates. He constantly shouted out encouragement to his pitcher. His uniform was always dirty because he would dive for ground balls hit between first and second base. But most remarkable of all, he talked to everybody. He talked to the umpires. He talked to an opponent who might be on second base. When he came to bat, he talked to the catcher, and, if he reached first base, he'd talk to the first baseman.

After high school, Paul and Jim spent the next four years living together as roommates in college. A few years later Jim was the best man in Paul's wedding. What Paul admired in his opponent in high school became the foundation for a life-long friendship.

Arm wrestling was a frequent activity among Native Americans. They viewed their opponent in such contests as someone who was offering his strength as a means to allow them to get stronger. In that sense, it was a cooperative competition.

Walnut Middle School in Grand Island, Nebraska, has developed a unique post-game ritual that formally honors opponents. After each contest, the Walnut Middle School teams gather quickly to select one or two opposing players who demonstrated outstanding sportsmanship or teamwork. The Walnut captains then present a small ribbon to those deserving opponents.

Top 20 coaches know that their opponents offer challenges and opportunities to develop physically and mentally. They also offer friendships that are built on mutual respect and can last for a lifetime. Top 20 coaches help students recognize and admire qualities in the opponents with whom they compete.

**Hey, how'd ya do? Did you appreciate anything about your opponent?**

## 9. HOW'D YA DO: DID YOU DEVELOP ANY STAR QUALITIES?

When we do training with high school groups, Willow will invite the biggest and strongest football player in the group to come up on stage. She then informs him that each of them will get into a football stance and, on the count of three, ram into each other and try to bowl each other over. The student, of course, is skeptical of doing this to a smaller woman, but Willow insists. They take their position and Willow begins to count. When she gets to two, she stands up, looks at the kid and says, "No way are we going to do this. You would crush me! Now here is the point. You have been training for years to ram into people on a football field. That is a skill needed in your sport. However if you do that when you are 25 years old in a grocery store, you'd be arrested. What you have been practicing for years is actually illegal the moment your football career is over. So there must be other reasons we want you to learn these football skills.

Top 20 coaches know that blocking and tackling skills are of no value to young people once they stop playing football. However, the Star Qualities that students can attain in sports and co-curriculars are valuable for a lifetime. Top 20 coaches help students develop some of the following internal strengths, social skills and problem solving skills that can make a positive difference in their lives during their school years and beyond.

- Self-confidence: believing in myself and my abilities
- Risk-taking: taking the difficult road to expand my comfort zone
- Responsibility: being dependable; someone others can count on
- Self-discipline: taking control of myself
- Flexibility: adapting to change and the stress created by it
- Toughness: dealing with adversity when things aren't going my way
- Courage: responding in spite of fear or lack of confidence
- Commitment: putting forth my full effort
- Fun: realizing that learning and working with others can be joyful
- Acceptance: valuing diversity and people who are different than I am
- Teamwork: helping others succeed; working well with others
- Focus: keeping my attention on the task or goal
- Persistence: sticking with the job until it is finished
- Patience: realizing that success often doesn't come easily
- Resourcefulness: finding a way to get the job done

One of the most important Star Qualities young people need to develop in order to succeed is **asking for help.** Students avoid asking for help because it appears to be a sign of weakness or inadequacy. However, few successes in life are attained solely on the qualities and talents of a single individual. Success requires help from others. Top 20 coaches model this Star Quality by making their own need of help from others obvious to their students.

Star Qualities are not skills or habits that develop overnight. They don't happen in one practice, concert or competitive event. Rather, they are developed over time. Top 20 coaches, concerned about the formation and potential of their students, make Star Qualities goals to be achieved by the youngsters in their care. They don't just hope that students might pick up a few Star Qualities along the way. They are as intentional in developing these skills and habits in students as they are in developing the backstroke in swimming, the wrist shot in hockey or writing headlines for the school newspaper.

Top 20 coaches actually have two names for their sport or activity: the traditional name and the Star Quality name.

    Examples:  Wrestling = Commitment
                   Marching Band = Teamwork
                   Soccer = Responsibility
                   Drama = Risk-taking

Numerous Star Qualities can obviously be developed in any sport or activity. The important thing is to make students aware that, whenever they are participating in a sport or activity, they should be on the lookout for opportunities to develop Star Qualities.

**Hey, how'd ya do? Did you develop any Star Qualities?**

## IS THAT ALL THERE IS?

Those of us who grew up in the 60s probably remember a song by Peggy Lee entitled *Is That All There Is?* The song tells the story of a young woman's disillusionment about life experiences.

Top 20 coaches don't allow their students to end their sporting or co-curricular experiences with the sentiment, "Is that all there is? Is it just about winning or losing?" Rather, if they have been associated with a Top 20 coach, young people will walk away from these activities with a profound sense of gratitude for the wonderful life lessons, personal awareness, relationships and qualities that they will carry into the rest of their lives.

**Hey, is that all there is?**
**No, there is so much more.**

# TIME FOR REFLECTION & ACTION

1. How can you lead students to get the most out of their athletic or co-curricular activities?

   A. How can you help them get the most out of winning and losing?

   B. How can you enhance their opportunities to have fun?

   C. How can you teach them important life lessons?

   D. How can you promote the goal of ongoing improvement?

   E. How can you communicate the importance of helping others succeed?

   F. How can you encourage them to conduct themselves well?

   G. How can you instill in students the desire to do their best?

H. How can you foster in them an appreciation for their opponents?

I. What Star Qualities can students develop by participating in your sport or co-curricular activity? How will you make this happen?

2. How can you communicate to parents or others in your school community the broader benefits available to students participating in your activity?

3. What did you become aware of while reading this chapter regarding an action you would like to take? What action would you like to take?

# CHAPTER 17

## Top 20 Coaches
# Are Gate Keepers of the Dream

Jack, a first-grader, sat on the front step of his house. He wore a cap with his favorite team's logo on the front and a jersey with his favorite player's name on the back. Pounding a ball into his baseball glove, he glanced up the street every few seconds. When he saw his dad's car turn the corner and head his way, Jack jumped up with excitement. As the car pulled into the driveway, the young lad ran to greet his father.

"Dad, can we play catch before supper?" asked Jack, who loved this nightly ritual.

"Sure thing, son," said his father as he caught Jack's first throw. "And after supper we'll go over to the park and watch the high school team play."

In various ways this scene is played out in countless families throughout the country. It may be a parent coaching a T-ball game, a mother driving neighborhood kids to soccer practice or a neighbor creating an ice rink in the back yard for kids to play hockey. It may be the family tail-gating before the local college's Saturday afternoon football game or dad's friends coming over to watch Tiger Woods at the Masters. It could even be a youngster lying in bed at night paging through *Sports Illustrated* magazine.

What is really taking place in each of these situations is that a dream is being formed. Youngsters are not just having fun when they play or watch sports; they are not only developing skills as they participate in athletic activities. They are also dream-making. Both the children and their parents create expectations for the future. They may dream of:

- Playing on the A-level traveling team.
- Starting on the varsity high school team.
- Just making the team to socialize with friends.
- Being named team captain.
- Making All-Conference or All-State.

- Getting a college scholarship.
- Becoming a pro athlete.
- Breaking scoring records.
- Making the decisive play in the championship game.

These dreams are formed over months and years of playing in the yard or at the park, attending athletic games in person or watching them on TV, or talking about sports with friends or family members. These dreams become real in the imagination of a kid who sits on his front step in uniform waiting for his father to come home from work.

Then, one day it's time for the dream to take on a new reality. It's time for the dream to pass through the *gate* of a child's imagination and manifest itself on a stage, field, pool, track or rink. Until now, the dream has resided in the child's imagination and, possibly, in his parents' imagination. But now the life and future of the dream is handed over to a person called *Coach*. It is the coach who will determine if the dream is allowed to pass through the gate and become a reality.

What will the coach decide?

- To cut the kid during tryouts or keep her on the team?
- To *start* the kid or keep him on the bench?
- To nominate her for All-Conference or not?

These and many other decisions that a coach makes will determine whether a dream is crushed or has a chance to become a reality.

## A COACH'S CONUNDRUM

Regarding the issue of dream-making, Top 20 coaches are aware of five certainties:

1. Youngsters and their parents are coming to them with a dream.

2. By necessity not all dreams can pass through the gate.

Some youngsters and their parents may have developed extremely unrealistic dreams. The dream may have seemed plausible while the kid was playing in the backyard, but, as he enters into a larger talent pool, he may not be as skilled as others.

Dream-making by a kid would not become a problem if she was the only one in the community developing a dream. The problem exists because many kids in the community are forming similar dreams that are on a collision course with each other. As soon as six kids dream of starting on the high school basketball team, someone's dream is going to be shattered.

3. It is a coach's responsibility to decide which dreams pass through the gate.

4. No matter how a coach handles the situation of denying a dream from passing through the gate (dream-breaking), the kid and his parents will experience some degree of disappointment.

5. There is a Top 20 way of handling dream-breaking.

## TOP 20 DREAM-BREAKING

As coaches, we would prefer that every kid's dream could become a reality. However, since that is not realistic, how can we best handle dream-breaking situations.

1. **Clarify Expectations:** By clarifying our expectations in advance, we might help youngsters and their parents develop more realistic dreams. In addition, we ought to have students and parents clarify their expectations to us. By understanding their expectations from the beginning, we will be aware of decisions we are making that are dream-breaking. Consequently, we can be more supportive during these times.

2. **Be Fair:** Because we are often making decisions that are selecting some kids over other kids, our process ought to be fair. We can best assure this if we communicate our selection process with others in our profession (other coaches or athletic directors), parents or students, and ask them for feedback on the fairness of the process. When we are making decisions that will result in someone's disappointment, we might ask that person if she thinks the process was fair.

3. **Focus on Team and Individual Youngster:** As a coach, it is our responsibility to be concerned about each player and the team as a whole. The parents' responsibility, however, is to focus on their own child. If both the parents and coaches are aware of these differences, we can be more respectful of each other's unique role.

4. **Demonstrate Positive 'Bedside Manner':** Statistics demonstrate that most doctors who are sued for malpractice have poor bedside manner. They may be competent with the medical aspect (IQ) of their profession, but they lack the human relationship dimension (EQ) of their pro-

fession. By communicating You Matter to our players and their parents, we create a greater level of trust and respect. Even though we may make decisions that break their dreams, they realize our genuine concern for the youngster. We might demonstrate this by checking in with the kids a few weeks later to see how they are doing.

5. **Guide to Other Activities:** Although we may make a dream-breaking decision, we may be able to guide the youngster to other community or school activities that would benefit him. We may even have another role on our team that he can fill and enjoy: student manager, statistician or game video-taper.

6. **Acknowledge Worth:** It is easy for youngsters who have developed dreams related to sports or other co-curricular activities to think of their worth as being determined by achievement or accomplishment. When their dreams have been broken, they can think of themselves as a failure. Top 20 coaches recognize the likelihood of this and find ways of communicating a youngster's worth even though she hasn't attained her dream. We can point out the Star Qualities we have recognized in the student that will help her be successful in future endeavors.

# TIME FOR REFLECTION & ACTION

1. Identify a dream you had as a youngster. How was your dream handled by a coach?

2. What makes dealing with a youngster's dream or a parent's dream difficult for you?

3. What can you do to respond to dream-breaking more effectively?

4. What did you become aware of while reading this chapter regarding an action you would like to take? What action would you like to take?

# CHAPTER 18

## Top 20 Coaches
# Get and Give Feedback Effectively

As the moderator of the middle school speech team, Mac met with his team after tournaments to analyze their performance. After one Saturday tournament, Mac approached Liam, who had struggled with his poetry recitation in the semifinals that day.

"Liam," he began, "you have got to make a decision. You have to decide whether or not you are going to commit time to prepare for these meets. You were not ready today and that was a big factor in our team's poor performance."

After first refusing to make eye contact with his coach, Liam turned defensive. "Well, you never even practiced once with me all week," he said. "You expect more from us than you do from yourself."

Mac was taken aback, but quickly recognized that he had taken a Bottom 80 approach with Liam. "Let's start over," he proposed. "How about this? I think I have something to share with you that might be helpful concerning your speech today. Would you be interested in hearing it?" Liam looked instantly relieved, nodded his head and listened attentively as his coach gave him feedback about the poem he had read.

**Feedback fuels the constant growth that Top 20s seek.** Effective coaches give their participants meaningful, necessary feedback to be more successful in their respective activities and lives.

Airplanes flying from Point A to Point B travel directly on course approximately 2%

of the time. However, because pilots are constantly receptive and responsive to helpful feedback from Air Traffic Control, they end up at the desired destination. A pilot unwilling to consider such feedback would certainly encounter dire consequences at some point in her career.

Why is feedback from Air Traffic Control so helpful to a pilot? Air Traffic Control has information that the pilot does not have: the exact location and destination of the plane, up-to-the-minute weather conditions and the location of other planes. Like pilots, Top 20 coaches are open to feedback. Their air traffic controllers include supervisors, student participants, parents and peers who can be helpful in keeping them on course towards their destination.

## TYPES OF FEEDBACK

Feedback comes in two forms: affirming and critical. Affirming feedback essentially says, "Don't change. You are doing fine." Critical feedback, on the other hand, says, "Change. You would be better off if you did it differently." Critical feedback also means it's important.

Rarely does ground control offer affirming feedback to pilots: "You are flying so perfectly today. Keep it up, Captain." More often, ground control's feedback would sound more like: "Change altitude to 31,000 feet now!"

Coaches and students need both forms of feedback to thrive. Listening to affirming feedback is quite easy: "You coached a great game last night. Your offensive strategy was very effective." Getting critical feedback is more challenging: "Your players lose confidence when you are yelling so much."

When coaches and students operate as Bottom 80s, they become defensive when critical feedback comes their way. The wall they put up to protect themselves prevents them from getting feedback that is in their best interest. When they are in Top 20 mode, they recognize that wall, are aware of the problem and attempt to lower their defensiveness. Top 20s know that critical feedback can only be helpful when they are open to it.

# GETTING FEEDBACK EFFECTIVELY

Knowing the importance of feedback, Top 20s know how to get it effectively for themselves. While it is not a specific, step-by-step route to success, they consider each part of the following process and apply what works best.

1. **Ask for feedback.** When we ask for feedback, we are more open and receptive and less defensive. Coaches who approach their own team members for feedback often discover things that can be easily altered or adjusted. This feedback can curtail major problems that are slowly developing within the team. Another source of feedback would be a mid-season meeting with the athletic director or supervisor.

2. **Listen openly and non-judgmentally.** Once we have lowered the wall by asking for critical feedback, we need to leave it down. We need to listen non-judgmentally without interrupting, disagreeing or countering with our own version of the situation. **Because we already know how we see it, this is the time to see how the other person sees it.** Questions at this point should only be asked to clarify what the other person is saying. Our listening does not mean that we agree but that we are seeking to understand.

3. **Paraphrase it back.** Once we receive the feedback, we ought to paraphrase it back to the provider. This will assure that we have clearly understood the person offering the feedback.

4. **Express thanks.** Giving critical feedback is an awkward and uncomfortable task for most people. Consequently, we should express gratitude to the person for doing what has probably been difficult and to encourage him to provide additional feedback in the future.

5. **Decide on the value of the feedback.** Having listened openly and non-judgmentally, it is now time to assess the value of the feedback. We may have received five different pieces of feedback from our players. After we assess the feedback, we may decide to take action on three of those ideas but determine that the other two may not warrant further attention at this point. We would then inform our players of what we plan to do.

# GIVING FEEDBACK EFFECTIVELY

Getting critical feedback is certainly an important part of personal and professional development, but giving critical feedback is also an important part of a coach's job. We serve as air traffic controllers for young people, hopefully guiding them safely to their intended destinations. Although it is not difficult to provide critical feedback, providing it **effectively** can be challenging.

Like Mac's example with his speech team, many advisors and coaches are more than willing to share their opinions and suggestions to young people. However, the feedback is ineffective when students protect themselves behind the wall of defensiveness. Bottom 80 coaches continue to offer feedback even though it goes unheeded by students. In order to be effective, Top 20 coaches consider the following steps in offering critical feedback.

1. **Establish rapport first.** Top 20s know that the defensive wall will not come down for strangers. Because human beings need to feel safe before they can be open, effective coaches form relationships with players by communicating You Matter and offering affirming feedback. Building trust is the first step to providing feedback effectively.

2. **Ask permission.** The best way to reduce defensiveness is to ask the person if we can offer feedback: "There's something I'd like to share with you that I think would be helpful. Would you like to hear it?" Often we offer our thoughts and ideas to someone who has not agreed to listen to them. If the person agrees, we should then ask, "Is now a good time for you?" Sometimes the other person might be open to listening but just not at that particular moment.

3. **Ask for the person's opinion.** Before providing feedback, ask how the student sees the situation. Let's say that a coach wants to talk to a player about coming late to practice. The coach might ask, "How do you think your coming late to practice affects our team?" The player's response will give the coach an idea of where she needs to go next.

4. **Offer direct feedback.** Once defensiveness has been minimized, we can offer direct meaningful feedback: "As a team we need to depend on each other. When you come late for practice and don't know what we're doing, your teammates can't rely on you."

5. **Look for agreement.** An oft-ignored part of the feedback process is to determine if any of the feedback made sense to the other person.

Tom often offered girls on his team feedback using the first four steps but neglected to get the player's agreement around any of the ideas he offered. He'd give feedback about shooting form but become frustrated when the player didn't even try to adopt any of his suggestions. With no agreement there is no buy-in. Consequently, he learned to ask, "Did you hear anything that you will take action on? When will you start?"

**T**RUE **T**ALES

6. **Offer follow-through and support.** We should offer feedback to students only if we are committed to do this final step with them. Bottom 80 coaches leave their players on their own after giving them feedback. Change is difficult. Our students need support and persistence, so we need to ask, "Can I check in with you about this again next week?"

## FINAL THOUGHTS

Timing is important. It would be absurd to go through these steps with an actor in the middle of a performance: "Hey, Romeo, I have something that might be valuable to share with you. How do you see your soliloquy going so far?" Before offering feedback we may have to wait until the next day's practice or a time that offers more privacy.

Top 20 coaches mentor other coaches. Bottom 80 coaches are often frustrated with the performance of their assistants, but never go to them with the feedback necessary to improve the situation. Head coaches have the responsibility of giving feedback to their assistant coaches as they develop their players and their own coaching careers. While this might be awkward at times, it is crucial to share helpful ideas with younger, less experienced coaches.

## TIME FOR REFLECTION & ACTION

1. Identify someone to whom you would like to give affirming feedback. What feedback do you want to give him or her?

2. Identify an individual or group from whom you would like to receive critical feedback. Consider the five steps for Getting Feedback Effectively (p. 156) before approaching these people for feedback.

3. Identify someone to whom you would like to give critical feedback. Consider the six steps for Giving Feedback Effectively (p. 157-158) before approaching this person.

4. What did you become aware of while reading this chapter regarding an action you would like to take? What action would you like to take?

Thank you for being a teacher and reading this book. Thank you for shaping the future by positively affecting the minds and hearts of America's youth.

Revolutions are filled with confusion and uncertainty, but they are fueled by a clear and passionate purpose. For us that purpose is to develop the potential in America's youth. Although this book doesn't have all the answers for the inevitable educational revolution, we hope it has raised some important questions that will foster professional conversations and effective practices vital to achieving that purpose.

As partners in this noble cause, we want to keep in touch with you. We want to listen to your stories, learn from your experiences and promote anything you discover that benefits our young people. Please email us at info@top20training.com with any anecdotes, questions or ideas that might yield *good change* for our students or ourselves. Visit our website at www.top20training.com to connect with other teachers who are joining the revolution.

With gratitude and appreciation,

Tom, Mary, Willow, Paul and Michael

# STAR QUALITIES*

## Internal Strengths

Self-confidence: believing in myself and my abilities

Risk-taking: taking the difficult road to expand my comfort zone

Self-motivation: getting myself started

Enthusiastic: having energy and interest for what I'm doing

Reflective: truly looking at myself

Reality based: dealing with what is in front of me

Emotionally aware: in touch with how my feelings influence my actions

Empowered: realizing that I'm in charge of my future

Responsible: being dependable; someone others can count on

Self-disciplined: taking control of myself

Flexible: adapting to change and the stress created by it

Toughness: dealing with adversity when things aren't going my way

Challenge: seeing problems as learning opportunities

Courageous: responding in spite of fear or lack of confidence

Commitment: valuing putting forth my full effort

Optimistic: hopeful, valuing the positive

Opportunistic: keeping my eyes and ears open for possibilities

Boundaries: accepting my limits and dealing with authority

## Social Qualities:

Fun: realizing that learning and working with others can be joyful

Respectful: honoring others by my words and actions

Acceptance: valuing diversity and people who are different than me

Communication: willing to listen to others and share appropriately

Honest: valuing living with truth and communicating truth

Empathetic: understanding what others are going through

Team player: helping others succeed

Open minded: accepting points of view different than my own

Conflict resolution: working through issues in a peaceful manner

Negotiate: using compromise and give-and-take in dealing with others

Tact: expressing myself with concern for other's feelings

Kindness: going out of my way to be nice and considerate of others

## Problem Solving Skills:

Time management: making good use of my time

Proactive: seeing what needs to be done and doing it

Focus: keeping my attention on the task or goal

Persistent: sticking with the job until it is finished

Patience: realizing that success often doesn't come easily

Organized: able to look ahead and keep my life in order

Logical: solving life's problems in a sensible, orderly manner

Values-oriented: knowing what is most important to my success

Goal setting: planning to meet long and short-term needs

Creative: inventive, full of ideas, able to see or do things in a new way

Practical thinking: using sound, reasonable judgment

Resourcefulness: finding a way to get the job done

Intellectual muscle: developing my thinking, stretching my mental abilities

Analysis: seeing the deeper meaning within

Synthesis: combining bits of information to find the greater meaning

*Developed by Peter Houseman, Jeanne Luken and Bob Goepel, Top 20 teachers at Mounds View Alternative Center, Mounds View, Minnesota.

# BIBLIOGRAPHY

Barker, Joel A. (1992). *Future Edge; Discovering the New Paradigms of Success.* New York, NY: William Morrow and Company Inc.

Bernabei, Paul, and others (2009). *Top 20 Parents: Raising Happy, Responsible and Emotionally Healthy Children.* New York, NY: Morgan James Publishing.

Bernabei, Paul, and others (2008). *Top 20 Teens: Discovering the Best-kept Thinking, Learning & Communicating Secrets of Successful Teenagers.* New York, NY: Morgan James Publishing.

Cashman, Kevin (1999). *Leadership From the Inside Out: Becoming a Leader for Life.* Provo, UT: Executive Excellence Publishing.

Covey, Stephen R. (1989). *The 7 Habits of Highly Effective People.* New York, NY: Simon and Schuster.

Frankl, Victor E. (1962, 1963). *Man's Search for Meaning.* Boston, MA: Beacon Press.

Glasser, William (1998). *Choice Theory: A New Psychology of Personal Freedom.* New York, NY: Harper-Collins.

Goleman, Daniel (1995). *Emotional Intelligence: Why It Can Matter More Than IQ.* New York, NY: Bantam Books.

Kuhn, Thomas S. (1970). *The Structure of Scientific Revolutions.* Chicago, IL: University of Chicago Press.

Mehrabian, Albert (1971). *Silent Messages.* Belmont, CA: Wadsworth.

Pransky, George S. (1991). *The Relationship Handbook: A Simple Guide to More Satisfying Relationships.* New York, NY: McGraw-Hill.

Rey, H. A. (2009). *Curious George.* Boston, MA: Houghton Mifflin Books for Children.

Satir, Virginia (1972). *Peoplemaking.* Palo Alto, CA: Science and Behavior Books, Inc.

Stoltz, Paul G. (1997, 1999). *Adversity Quotient – Turning Obstacles into Opportunities.* New York, NY: John Wiley and Sons, Inc.

Walsh, David (2004). *Why Do They Act That Way? A Survival Guide to the Adolescent Brain for You and Your Teen.* New York, NY: Free Press.

# TOP 20 TRAINING

Top 20 Training provides training and materials to empower youth and adults:

- To develop their potential
- To make a positive difference in their lives, relationships and experiences
- To make a positive difference in the lives of others

**Top 20 training sessions:** Top 20 training sessions are conducted throughout the United States for youth, educators, parents, coaches, social workers and other adults working in a wide variety of businesses, churches and organizations. For a schedule of Top 20 training sessions, go to www.top20training.com. To schedule a training session for your school or organization, contact Top 20 Training at info@top20training.com.

**Top 20 books:** *Top 20 Teachers: The Revolution in American Education*

*Top 20 Teens: Discovering the Best-kept Thinking, Learning & Communicating Secrets of Successful Teenagers*

*Top 20 Parents: Raising Happy, Responsible and Emotionally Healthy Children*

**Top 20 teacher manuals:** Teacher manuals include Top 20 classroom processes, detailed lesson plans for all concepts in the Top 20 Teens book and student handouts.

**Top 20 TLC Teacher Manual:** Grades 3-6
**Top 20 Teens Teacher Manual:** Grades 7-12

If you have questions about Top 20 Training or would like to order books or materials, contact Top 20 Training.

www.top20training.com        info@top20training.com        651-690-5758